Bumper Book of Storytelling into Writing – Key Stage 1

Bumper Book of Storytelling into Writing – Key Stage 1

Pie Corbett

Clown Publishing

First published in 2006 by
Clown Publishing
7 Ferris Grove, Melksham, Wiltshire SN12 7JW

A catalogue record for this book is available from the
British Library.

ISBN-10   0-9553008-0-0
ISBN-13   978-09553008-0-6

Cover design by Peter Hardy
Clown by Nicole – The Mead School, Trowbridge,
Wiltshire
Typesetting and Design by Dorwyn, Wells, Somerset
Printed and bound in Great Britain by 4edge Ltd, Hockley.

Contents

Introduction

What is this book?

This book is a resource bank for teachers at key stage 1 who are beginning to develop story-making as part of their curriculum. In the book, I have outlined the underlying principles and a range of teaching strategies as well as including a bank of stories for teachers to use. Whilst this may well be handy in saving time, I hope that teachers will develop other stories with their different classes and add these to their repertoire. The story telling strand fits in with an enriched language curriculum. For instance, children need to also tell stories (recounts) about their own lives because ultimately they will draw upon their own experience as well as their experience of stories to create their own tales.

The process of storymaking is a set of understandings that teachers have been developing over the last six years. It is not a rigid set of rules – and needs to be approached creatively and thoughtfully, adapting as new insights are gained.

Narrative is a primary act of mind

Storytelling is a natural human activity. The expectation that everyone should be able to write is only really a recent idea. The more we have worked on narrative, the more I have become aware that narrative is an essential way of thinking but also that humans are storymaking machines – it is a constant, natural thread through our lives. Starting with oral stories means that we are tapping into a natural process. Writing is tough – especially for many small children!

Why storymaking?

About six years ago almost every school I visited was struggling to raise standards in writing. Sometimes the children's writing was lagging way behind their reading ... and I began to wonder why this might be so. What I had noticed was that the best writers were always children who read avidly. It seemed obvious that these children had to be internalising narrative patterns – the language of stories – and then recycling them in their writing.

I knew that toddlers who were read to at home did this because I had noticed my own children recycling phrases from their reading. I began sharing this thought with teachers. It soon became obvious that there was a phase that all children who are read to regularly at home pass through. They alight upon a favourite story that they like to have read again and again (usually something thrilling like 'Topsy and Tim go shopping'). What is intriguing about this is that the children inevitably learn the whole story, word for word, through constant, repetitive rereading.

These children will then reuse some of the language that they have internalised – they start playing with the language. I remember Poppy, when she was only about two and a half, hearing a knock on the door and saying, 'Daddy, it's a little bit early for customers!' That was a direct quote from Granny Goggins – we were in the Postman Pat phase! I noticed too that it

Introduction

was easy enough to make stories up with Poppy – because she had a bank of structures, characters, settings and possibilities to draw upon and reuse.

This thinking lead onto the simple realisation that in order to write any text type, the writer has to be very familiar with it – and this comes most powerfully through repetitive rereading or being read to. Of course, small children do not read – they hear the language being read to them and often join in, saying the words aloud. This lead me onto the idea that a powerful way to internalise language patterns comes through 'hearing it' and 'saying it' – talking the text type.

Of course, if you want to write a text type it may well be that seeing it written down will also be of use. However, at this point the literacy strategy in England was emphasising the move from reading into writing – but not yet building in the importance of 'talking the text type'. I was meeting many teachers who felt that the reason that the writing was poor was because the children were unimaginative or watched too much TV! I was fast coming to the conclusion that what we needed to do was find strategies to help children internalise patterns of language that could then be called upon to help them compose. In other words, the issue was not so much a lack of the ability to imagine – but rather a lack of the building blocks with which to imagine.

I noticed that when teachers were teaching, they started with a model text and then moved into writing. The difficulty seemed to be that they did not loiter with the model for long enough – so that when the children came to write you could not see the underlying patterns in their writing.

The storymaking process begins with this idea of 'loitering' with the model text – finding strategies to make it memorable so that the text enters the child's long-term working memory – only moving on when the children really know the model well ... so well, that they have embedded the text in their minds – irrevocably and forever.

The idea of building a storehouse of stories inside the mind lies at the heart of storymaking. What would happen if in 'reception' children learned say ten simple stories – and then added in another ten in year 1. They would enter year two with about twenty stories to draw upon when writing.

The idea of 'internalising language patterns' lies at three different levels.

1. First of all there is the underlying narrative pattern – the big shape of the story – the story 'pathway'. Rather like internalising a writing frame. Over the last few years, it has become increasingly obvious that there are only a few underlying patterns that are constantly recycled.
2. Secondly, children internalise the flow of the sentences. The way in which sentences in stories are not the same as sentences in speech. For instance, a sentence might start with a preposition (*'across the road was an old house', 'in a distant valley lived a giant'*).
3. Finally, children internalise vocabulary – building up their store of language. In particular, gathering a broader bank of connectives with which to link and structure narrative patterns.

Introduction

Of course they are also internalising characters, settings and events – the sorts of things that might happen such as the sense that in a story something often goes wrong and has to be sorted out.

The point about hearing and telling stories is that this is the most powerful way of acquiring language – speaking and listening is how children learn language. The storymaking process aims to help children embed into their daily linguistic competence the structures that are needed for them to create narratives ultimately for themselves.

Whilst I was visiting schools, I began asking reception children if they knew any stories and very soon discovered that many children knew no stories – or if they did know some, they could not retell any as whole tales. Occasionally I would meet a child who would launch into a tale full of gusto and verve – and it was obvious that somebody had read to them or told them stories. I could hear the rhythm of the adult's telling coming through the child's voice.

Research I carried out at the 'International Learning and Research Centre' supported this, showing that on entry to school only 2% of children could retell a whole story. I am indebted to Mary Rose and the many teachers whom we worked with at the centre on the original research projects into Storymaking – which were funded by the DFES Innovations unit. The teachers contributed so generously, opening their classrooms and minds as we developed our thinking. I am grateful to all those who continue to contribute their thinking – especially to Mary for her wisdom, her enquiring mind and her focus upon setting up situations within which we could learn together. I have gathered further insights from groups across the country including teachers on the Isle of Wight, in Bradford, Denbighshire and elsewhere – all of whom have helped me shape my thinking as we have travel on this story journey.

The impact of the storymaking project is reflected in the new literacy framework, which now has a storytelling strand in every primary year. Though the importance of storytelling had already been recognised in the 'Writing Narrative' Flier that the National Literacy Strategy sent to every primary school back in 2001. (The flier came from some writing that I had done with the author David Almond (who wrote 'Skellig') for the key stage 3 strategy). We began by stating that *'story writing is magical – its appeal lies in the creation of imaginative worlds. Stories help us to enthral, to intrigue, to entertain, to wonder and to bring our world and ourselves alive. There is a strong cycle that links reading, discussing, telling, listening and writing ... The roots of story writing lie in a rich experience of listening to and watching stories, drama and role play, early story reading, frequent rereading of favourites and the telling/retelling of all forms of story'.* We then went on to introduce the following 'principle' that underpins narrative writing (and that this book explores in detail):

- *Imitation – early story composition can be based on well-loved tales.*
- *Innovation – encourage young writers to base their stories on known tales, making changes to characters, settings or events.*
- *Invention – as young writers acquire a good store of stories, they can mix the ingredients and invent their own.'*

Introduction

This book describes the process of building up the bank of stories. The approach is multi-sensory, primarily oral – learning stories by heart so that the children can retell them or call upon them to fashion new tales of their own. When telling the stories, children use actions and a story map as a visual reminder. There are of course other strategies to help children internalise language that need to run alongside storymaking – a rich vein of reading, poetry and rhyme, drama and play plus interactive talk are all essential.

There are three key skills to storymaking.

1. **Imitation** – this is the ability to learn stories so that the child has a bank of tales by heart. Indeed, the stories are known so well that they have become part of the long-term working memory, embedded into their linguistic competence.
2. **Innovation** – this is the ability to adapt a well-known story, in order to create a new story.
3. **Invention** – this is the ability to draw upon the full range of stories, and one's life, to create something new. There may well be elements from different tales as well as totally new ideas.

Finally

Over the last five years there has been an increasing interest in storymaking as an effective process that helps children build up their bank of stories and move into creating their own. Many schools across the country and abroad have been using the approach and discovering that it can release creativity – because you cannot create out of nothing! Children who know no stories will not be able to create their own ... the bigger the resource to draw upon, the more creative children can be.

Again and again, we have seen children's writing improve – often radically because at long last they have a story to tell. There have also been occasions when children with (so-called) special needs gain confidence and lead the class in storytelling. Progress can be startling. If you want to know if it is working then record a few children before you start, asking them the question, 'Can you tell me a story?' After several weeks of storymaking ask the question again – and listen to the difference. If the teaching is thorough and engaging you will find that children move from having no tale to tell to being able to retell a whole story – and older pupils will add in their own variations to make it their own.

The process is simple enough and it fits easily and naturally into good infant practice. Soon it becomes an easy part of the everyday routine. The impact can be quite dramatic – so keep at it!

Let's create together schools, which have stories at their heart – for without them, we have heartless schools. It is worth remembering that at the heart of every culture lies song, dance, art, religion ... and stories. Without the arts, we have no heart, no culture and our schooling becomes dry dust upon the wind.

Chapter 1 Learning Stories

The first stage (often referred to as 'imitation') is to help the children build up the bank of stories. This should be easy and quite natural – the teacher telling a story and the children gradually joining in until they know the story by heart – until the story is in their long-term working memory and will burn their like a flame forever.

Which story?

Choose a story that you enjoy and that you think the children will enjoy. I have provided a bank of well-known tales that most teachers would use at key stage 1. However, you may well be lucky enough to have children whose heritage is from other parts of the world and they or their families may also have other stories to share. As children move through the primary school, they need to acquire the most common traditional tales of our culture but also broaden this bank out to include tales from many other cultures. Without the common traditional tales from a culture, children cannot take part in that culture – they are cut off from one of the roots of that culture. Interestingly, children soon discover that every culture will share the same sorts of stories – because we are all human.

Teaching the children the stories

The story that you have chosen will need to be told every day, possibly several times, using actions and a story map or board. This does not have to become a great song and dance – after all, how long does it take to retell the Gingerbread Man!

It is important to keep retelling the chosen story daily. Our experience suggests that after several weeks, the children will know it really well. The aim is to make sure that the story becomes burned into their memories.

Story maps

After you have told the story once then draw a story map in front of the children. The maps need to be simple and very clear so that they capture the plot in one go – and can act as a visual reminder. Remember to show on the map a simple pathway through the story – a dotted line or single line with an arrow should suffice.

The map needs to be on a large sheet of sugar paper and displayed at the front where it can be seen. Keep the map displayed while the children are learning the story. Ultimately, maps can be laminated and placed in a storymap rack at the side of the room. These can then be used at any time for revisiting stories.

Once you have drawn the map and then used it for a second telling, it is worth the children drawing their own maps. At key stage 1, it is probably worth the children just copying your map though more mature children may add extra words or images to help them recall the story. The act of having to reprocess the story and represent it in a different form helps to make the tale memorable in their minds ... if you want children to remember something then the more they 'do' with it, in different ways, the more likely they will be to remember it.

Year 2 children might keep a topic book of story maps that could move with them into year 3. After all, maps can be used at any level and revisited to create new stories.

Not all stories lend themselves to maps – though maps are good because they are so visual. You may need to use a storyboard, story mountain or flow chart. Whatever you do – provide a simple visual reminder, which will be very handy for those who think visually. Some teachers also use objects from the story such as puppets or pictures – all acting as visual prompts. This can be very useful for those for whom English is a new language. Though ultimately, you will want the children to 'imagine' and 'see' the story in their minds.

Actions

Whilst using story maps, objects or pictures helps to provide a visual prompt, actions that accompany the story also provide a kinaesthetic reminder that makes the language and tale more memorable as well as helping the children understand what is happening. Actions can be used to show events and are often made up by the children. However, the key connectives should have fixed actions so that in each class the children revisit connectives and build up a bank that they can call upon for their own storymaking.

It is worth reminding ourselves that language is not just words – it is also rhythm and action. If you watch a French speaker, you soon notice that the speech is accompanied by actions! Language and action are interlinked.

When telling stories the children will be using typical narrative connectives *(Once upon a time, one day, first, next, after that, suddenly, finally)*. It is also handy if the teacher revisits some of the language features during the course of everyday classroom activities, e.g. *'This afternoon we have four things to do. First ..., next ..., after that ... Finally, we will have a story ... '*.

Whole class retelling

Some teachers are worried that retelling the same story might become a bit boring. On one hand this may be so – but it is worth thinking about how much human beings like to revisit the same patterns. For instance, I have been listening to 'The Beatles' for over 30 years and still enjoy their songs. In a logical sense, this is ridiculous. I know what is going to happen; I know the songs word for word, note for note. So why is it that I keep on listening and enjoy hearing such familiar patterns?

Perhaps in order to survive, we need the comfort of patterning in our lives – otherwise the world would be a random blur of events. So – humans categorise, label and create patterns so that the world becomes something we understand and life is a series of routines and patterns without which we could not survive. Think how disturbing it can be when our daily routines are destroyed. Patterning is a fundamental comfort and coping device for humans. Narrative helps to provide basic patterns. Narrative is a template that we put upon life in order to explain our experiences to ourselves – and ourselves to the world.

You may find that after a while, you will want to ring the changes and find different ways to enliven and vary whole class retellings. Try the following ideas:

- all saying the story together;
- just girls or just boys;
- all those in blue/red/green ...
- a group or pair lead the class;
- an individual sits in the teacher's 'storytelling' chair;
- a child leads the class wearing story cloak or hat;
- tell the story in different ways – loudly, softly, silently, just miming the actions, or very rapidly – babble gabble.

Withdrawing from telling

When you first tell a story to a class, you will be leading the way. Encourage the children to join in until they are saying every word with you. It is important that you then gradually withdraw from telling because you want the children to become independent. The more that you dominate the telling, the more that some children rely on you. Indeed, some children may never join in at all because you are doing all the work – they will just sit there passively, watching what you are doing.

However, this is not a 'performance' of story telling – the aim is for the children to learn the story. Once you have told it through several times, the children will begin to pick up on the most memorable parts – often the rhythmic, repetitive parts, the dialogue and the explosive dramatic bits. Keep going until the children are joining in with everything.

Once they seem confident, you can start to withdraw from saying the words – maybe you can just mouth the words or just keep prompting with the actions. If the children falter in their telling, you can always leap in and keep the story going. The aim is to move from you being the dominant teller to becoming a listener. The children move from being listeners to becoming tellers.

Teacher as teller	Withdraw and prompt	Teacher as listener
Children as listeners	Increasingly join in	Children as tellers

Learning stories

Story Circles

As the children become increasingly confident in telling the story in a whole class setting, you can move into story circles. The children sit in a small circle and try telling the story simultaneously. It is worth making sure that there is always an adult with story circles at the start to ensure that they do not loose their way. If they do not know the story well enough, they may slip into a string of sentences linked endlessly with 'and then'. The adult should not dominate the group but sit on the edge, ready to prompt if the children lose their way. Make sure too that the children can see their story maps.

Story Pairs

Only move to pairs, when you are fairly convinced that the children have the story in their long-term memory – this will take longer than you imagine. If you rush into pairs too quickly then the children will not know the story sufficiently well enough to retell it. Indeed, you may well have to stay at the level of whole class retelling until you have become pretty fed up with the story! The skill is for the teacher to dress up the whole class retelling in different ways – keeping it fun and lively.

Pairs can operate in three different ways. The first stage is for the children to retell together. They need to sit facing each other and stare into each other's eyes. They tell and perform the actions at the same time like a mirror. Their story maps could be placed on the ground in front of them. You will have to model how to work as a pair, showing them exactly what to do.

The second stage is for the tellers to take it in turns telling the story bit by bit. Often this will be sentence by sentence. A third stage is for the children to tell it in two halves – with the partner who is not telling ready to act as a prompt.

Pairs can be teamed up with pairs of children from other classes to retell their story. This provides an incentive and an audience for the retelling – after all, the point of learning a story is to tell it to someone else!

What about those who do not join in?

There are often a few children who do not join in. They sit on the carpet and just look at you – as if you had been beamed down from planet Zog. Look out for these children – the challenge will be to find ways to encourage them to participate. Are they actually internalising the story?

Sometimes this is just a lack of confidence and gradually, with plenty of encouraging smiles, they will join in. Some children may need reminding to join in. Others may need an adult to sit beside them and encourage them. Some may need to work in a smaller group or a pair with an adult. Often using puppets or finger puppets can help less confident children as the attention is taken away from the child and placed onto the puppet. You may well find that you have a child who has been worrying you – then one day Mum comes in and starts telling you how much they have been enjoying the retellings at home!

Preparing to tell a story

The first time you tell a story without a book can be quite daunting. The usual panic is that you will forget the words – so solid preparation will pay off. Here are the basic steps:

1. Find your story.
   You could use a story from the bank in this book just to get you going or you may have a favourite of your own. Start with something simple so that you – and the children – gain confidence. Don't worry – the second story will be easier to learn – because you are exercising a part of the brain that you may not have used too often – also because you are developing memory and strategies for learning a chunk of text. In the appendices I have listed various suggestions for useful sources for stories – though the early ladybird books of traditional tales provide a pretty good bank.

2. Adapt the story.
   I always rewrite the story. Partly because the rewriting helps me learn the tale – the act of reprocessing it through my brain and onto the page helps me to memorise it. But also because I want to build in certain sentence patterns and vocabulary (especially connectives) so that these are repeated enough to become part of the children's linguistic competence (see the language bank in the appendices).

3. Draw the map.
   I always draw a map before going anywhere near the classroom. This is important because it is not easy to come up with a simple, effective visual representation of a plot. The process of simplifying the story into its key incidents that will appear on the map also helps me to internalise the pattern of the tale (see appendices for an example).

4. Practice.
   I put the story onto a tape or burn it onto a CD so that I can play it in the car or on my Ipod. When I record the story, I do it line by line leaving a space in between each sentence. I make sure that the space is long enough for me to repeat the sentence. So – the recording teaches me. It says a sentence – I repeat it in the gap. As I begin to feel that I might know a bit – I turn off the recording and try saying it aloud. I keep doing this until I know it pretty well.

5. Build in actions.
   The final element is to make sure that I have thought through the actions. It is worth having certain actions that stay the same – the key connectives for example (see appendices for suggested actions). However, some actions can be made up with the class, providing ownership of the story.

Learning stories

Telling a story for the first time

This can be nerve wracking but once you have got over any initial qualms most people find storytelling enormous fun. Here are a few tips that may help you:

- have a map just beside you to glance at;
- pin a map on the wall behind the children so that if you get lost you can glance over the children's heads;
- have the script beside you to glance at;
- have the bare bones of the story on a prompt card;
- tell the tale with a partner – one of you reading from the script.

Once you have told the story once – then you are fine. Because the next time the children will put you right ... 'you didn't say that last time', is a very handy prompt! The truth is that after a while, you will have your own class version that you tell together and the story falls into its own pattern.

When you are telling a story, take time to settle children on the carpet – make sure that you can see everybody's eyes. As you tell the story, keep looking round, scanning the group and drawing them in with your eyes. Make your eyes larger and use expression. Vary the pace, using dramatic pauses as well as varying the volume. If anyone looks scared, tone the tale down. You may build in simple refrains or start with a short rhyme. Sometimes I use a musical instrument at the start and end – just to get everyone listening.

Understanding the story

Of course, chanting a story is one thing – indeed, if you are not careful a rhythmic chanting may actually be meaningless. The story needs to be told with expression and variation to bring it alive. If you are working with children for whom English is a new language or with those who might struggle with some of the vocabulary, then you may need extra prompts such as objects or pictures. This makes the learning of vocabulary simple, sensible and fun.

Making it memorable

There are many different ways in which a story can be made memorable. Daily retelling is important but that in itself may not be sufficient for some children – especially those who do not learn so powerfully in an auditory manner.

Given a story such as the Gingerbread Man, most teachers can begin to generate a suite of activities that might help to make the tale memorable as well as capitalising on the children's interests – baking gingerbread, writing recipes, making a large wall map of the journey, hot seating the characters, painting pictures and making models all spring to mind as possibilities. It is worth asking ourselves – what are the key activities that really help the

Learning stories

children internalise the story? Of course, other activities may well spring out of the story and be part of the broader curriculum.

In the story bank, I have provided a few simple suggestions for each story – though I have no doubt that you will also think of other activities. Generally speaking, the more you do with a story – the more it is reprocessed in the mind in different ways, the more memorable it becomes. It is worth devising a multi-sensory programme so that they children have activities that open each channel for learning as well as opportunities to 'play' at the story:

Visual – paint, draw, model and watch the story;

Auditory – hear and say the story, discussing, retelling, drama;

Cognitive – memory tricks, discussions, key connectives;

Kinaesthetic – drama, role-play, dance, model making, building.

Think **VACK** when planning, making sure that you have built in opportunities for stories to be represented through art in a visual manner, through drama in a kinaesthetic way as well as retelling and thinking about the story.

Providing an audience for the story

In the hurly burly of learning the story, it is easy to lose sight of the whole purpose of storytelling – to communicate a story to someone else. It is always worth building into the programme of activities some sort of chance to retell to a new audience:

- whole class assembly performance;
- capture the story on video/digital camera and show to other classes on interactive board;
- class, group or paired retelling to other classes;
- make a CD of retellings and sell to community.

One reception class uses a mini recorder as a regular part of their storymaking. The children learn a story and then retell it into the recorder. This means that they can listen to their own retelling – which has the result of the children hearing their own telling becoming their own audience. It becomes a simple way of assisting oral redrafting.

Story boxes, felt boards and puppets

This can be quite a fun activity but also acts as a powerful visual representation of a story. The boxes can simply contain objects from the story. Your boxes could be simple shoeboxes – decorated – and inside will be your story items. Or the boxes can have two sides cut off so that a simple 'room' or scene can be created using small items of doll's furniture, etc. The children can use these when they are playing at storymaking.

Learning stories

Felt boards are something that I remember with fondness from my own childhood and can act as a stimulus to storymaking. Large puppets, finger and stick puppets are all part of the storymaking classroom. These provide a real stimulus for play and retelling to an audience (see resources).

Drama and storytelling

Drama is a natural accompaniment to storymaking. It helps children get to know the text really well – often having to listen again to and reuse parts of the text. Drama activities are especially useful for encouraging a return to the original story to internalise the patterns and develop an interpretation ... Also, drama can help children begin to generate new ideas for their own inventions.

- **Dressing up clothes** – it is worth building up a bank of dressing up clothes for each story.
- **Hot seating** – interviewing characters from a story.
- **Freeze frames** – creating a frozen tableau from a key moment in a story.
- **Miming scenes** – miming a scene from a story. Can the others guess which scene? Miming what might happen next.
- **Role-playing** – revisit scenes or imagine new ones.
- **Free role-play** – providing a play area such as a bears' cave or Grandma's cottage complete with dressing up clothes acts as a simple invitation to 'play at' the story.
- **Act the story** – works well if the teacher narrates the story as the children act it out.
- **Puppet theatre** – finger or stick puppets (or felt boards).
- **Journalists** – interviewing the story characters.
- **'News' programmes** – pretending to be interviewers and putting on the 'News' – interviewing the Goats about the Troll.
- **Monologues** – draw an outline of the character and add on speech bubbles – what is he/she thinking and feeling? Teacher needs to demonstrate how to 'think aloud' revealing a character's 'thoughts in the head'.
- **Gossip** – 2 characters chatting about what is happening.
- **Phone calls** – mobile phone calls from a character to a friend.
- **Statements to police** – does the troll have a defence??
- **Writing in role** – in role write a letter to a friend, a diary entry or a newspaper report about what is happening.
- **Objects or costumes** – telling the tale of the character, or placing an object from a story in the centre of the group to then decide what should happen.
- **Forum theatre** – a scene is set up. The action can be paused and audience members suggest what might happen next.
- **Role on the wall** – someone lies down on sheets of paper – an outline is drawn plus comments, quotes, suggestions.

Learning stories

- **Timeline invention** – draw a timeline or story mountain – children then have to add in the key events in a story – and use this for telling.

Making storytelling special

There are a number of simple 'extras' that help to create a storymaking classroom. Displays are obvious – but what about:

- **Storyteller's hat** – a fancy hat for telling.
- **Storyteller's chair** – dress up the chair.
- **Storyteller's cloak** – velvet and shimmering stars!
- **Magic Carpet** – a flight to story world.
- **Story Music** – to establish atmosphere.
- **Story lights** – a star shape or crescent moon.
- **Story box or bag** – for puppets or secret objects.

Creating a storymaking area

Ideally, every classroom needs an area where children can play at storymaking. This might be a 'Storytelling Castle' – a large card castle – and inside the teacher could put a cloak, chair, hat, mat and small storymaps for storytelling. It might also contain writing equipment, puppets or felt figures. In the area, children could retell stories they know, innovate on stories and create new ones. If they have worked on a new story then, when they are ready, they could tell it to the class.

Discussing the story

A key factor in helping children understand the story will be discussing what happens. Questioning is important and it does help if this does not sink to the level of the teacher firing comprehension questions like some sort of verbal reasoning test. The phrase 'tell me' as an invitation to discuss reading was first introduced to me by Aidan Chambers in his excellent book titled 'Tell me'. Begin by asking the children to 'tell you' what they liked, disliked, any puzzles or patterns. These four areas will often open up some discussion between the children. Make sure that you show interest in the children's ideas so that you model being a good listener.

It is also worth being aware of the importance of asking questions that do not just rely on simple retrieval and description. Move on to questions that involve deduction and inference – perhaps asking how someone might have felt where it is not obviously stated in the text. Of course, drama activities such as hot seating all help to deepen children's understanding of a story by putting them into different character's shoes.

Learning stories

Daily retelling

I cannot stress enough the importance of retelling the story daily. You do not have to make a great fuss and a do about this but memorable repetition is very important in language learning. If you drop the process for a while because Christmas has struck then don't blame me if the children struggle!

Revisiting old favourites

It is worth having a story bag or box. For every story that you learn, pop a fluffy toy into the bag to represent the story. This means that every now and then you can get the bag out and someone can choose a story to retell. In this way the bank of tales is cumulative – the first is not lost but by the time we reach the summer term we have a bank of 6 to 10 stories that we know well.

Storytime

Some teachers have moved on to holding a special 'storytime' every day. This can be very helpful in schools where language learning is an issue. 'Storytime' might last about half an hour and consists of different aspects of story. One year two teacher holds 'storytime' daily and includes such activities as:

- read a new picture book to the class and discuss;
- reread an old favourite;
- sing an action rhyme;
- read a new poem;
- whole class retelling of an old favourite;
- retell story being learned;
- teacher makes up a new story with suggestions from the children.

Poems and rhymes

Sadly, there are many children who only know a smattering of rhymes – if any – on entry to school. Given what we now know about the link between rhyme and reading and spelling, it seems that this too is an important area to develop. Indeed, many children only seem to know 'Bob The Builder'!

A simple way to begin to build up a bank of poems and rhymes would be to introduce a 'poetry journal'. Each week/fortnight a new rhyme is pasted into the book. The journal goes home with the children – and it is not for the child to read but it is for the adult to 'do' with the child. This is a handy way of involving parents or carers constructively in building up the storehouse of language and images.

Learning stories

The idea is for the parent to sing or chant or play the rhyme daily. The rhyme is also the 'rhyme of the week' in class. By the end of the week most of the children should have added another rhyme to their repertoire. Again this needs to be cumulative – dipping back into old favourites so that they are not lost.

Start with nursery rhymes – then move into action rhymes, skipping, clapping and circle songs (my anthology The Works Key Stage 1 has many of these – see resources). Once again it is the systematic, repetitive element that helps the children acquire the rhymes.

Parents

Involving parents in storymaking is the next obvious step for any storymaking class or school. There are many different ways in which this might occur. Many schools now have banks of tapes, CDs and story sacks that can be borrowed and used at home. We also hold sessions for parents and carers to learn about sharing books with children. This is something that we have to keep at relentlessly – every new batch of children brings a new group of parents. I well recall one parent who attended a session about the importance of reading to children, saying afterwards that she wished she had known this for her first child.

Story telling workshops, where parents are taught how to tell stories, would be useful. These could be lead by teachers or where possible by community members, so that different groups can learn stories from different communities, enriching everyone's story storehouse. Stories could also be put onto tapes, or CDs – either by an adult or by children. These might be handy for car journeys – or last thing at night.

Parents and carers too need to know how to build up a bank of 'family' stories as well as traditional tales – those stories about things that have happened in a family. Stories about trips, relatives and things that happen in everyday life ... *'Tell us the story about when we ...'*

A storymaking school

A storymaking school would have a strong commitment to reading, writing, performing – there would be storymaking areas and every class would have magical mats, hats, cloaks ... there might be a story giant's chair in the playground or a mini forum for performance ... there would be story maps and everywhere you go – children telling stories or watching performances. Drama and puppet groups would be a regular occurrence and so too would visits from authors. There would be homemade books by classes and children. Projects would spring out of stories. Narrative would be a living thing – central to children's lives.

Chapter 2 Changing stories

The second stage in storymaking is where you take a well-known story and change it a bit to make it your own (often called 'innovation). This is a traditional approach to storymaking that has gone on for thousands of years. For instance, Shakespeare wrote 39 plays ... and only 3 of them were original, the rest were all innovations on well-known tales!

In the main, nearly all writing in primary schools is innovation – you can usually spot the underlying patterns ... In fact, if I look back at the stories that I was writing when I was about ten years old, it was pretty obvious what I was reading – all my stories involved 3 children and a dog named scamp – holiday, cave, treasure, nasty villain appears, hide, police at last moment, steaming mug of cocoa and reward. The end. Yes – I was an Enid Blyton innovator!

Actually, as you become more used to looking at the underlying patterns in narratives, you begin to notice how the same sorts of patterns reoccur. Indeed, many people would suggest that there are only a few patterns constantly recycled. Christopher Hampton in 'The Seven Basic Plots' suggests there are only seven. We will return to this idea when we look at the third stage of 'invention'.

It is worth bearing in mind that the idea of 'innovation' is based on how children learn language. Initially, they imitate the sound patterns that they hear repetitively used in certain contexts. This is often rewarded by the parents' delight so they repeat the 'word' again. As the child builds a vocabulary, innovations appear. The most obvious example is the way in which young children generalise the past tense principle and add 'ed' on where it doesn't quite work – I 'goed' down the lane. When children innovate, it is a sign of language growth – the brain has generalised the principle and is trying to apply it into new situations.

It is worth reminding ourselves at this point that it is important not to move on to innovation until the original story is well embedded within the children's long-term working memory. The yardstick for this is whether they can retell it independently. If you move on too quickly then the results will disappoint. The teacher has to beware of the curriculum's desire to encourage you to dash on, 'delivering' objectives with scant regard for whether anyone has learned anything. Storymaking schools have learned that for many children slowing down and learning thoroughly through imaginative repetition is a surer way of securing genuine progress.

Innovation is harder than imitation – at first! It really has to be taught ... the quality of the children's innovations is a direct reflection of the quality of the teacher's innovation. There are 5 basic possibilities – though often these intermingle.

1. **substitution** – making simple changes;
2. **addition** – retelling the same story but adding in more;
3. **alteration** – retelling the same story but making significant changes that have repercussions;
4. **change of viewpoint** – retelling the same story but from a different angle;
5. **recycling the plot** – reusing the underlying plot and theme but in a totally different context.

Changing stories

These five stages are hierarchical – in so far as they become increasingly sophisticated. Most reception classes will be able to accomplish a simple 'substitution' but by the end of the year may well be adding in some extra description or events.

However, a confident year two class may well be altering events, adding in much more description or even retelling a tale from a different character's viewpoint. They might reuse the underlying plot to create a totally new story.

The beauty of this approach is that it makes differentiation easier. Some children in a year 2 class will be retelling with a few simple substitutions – whilst others may be adding in detail or making significant alterations. What is essential is that the teacher ensures that ultimately the children's compositions are supported by the original telling but also allow them to make progress. A confident year two should not just be doing a simple substitution! Let us take a closer look at the five categories:

1. Substitutions

This is the easiest form of innovation. A few simple changes can provide a sense of ownership and accomplishment for the youngest and least confident. For those who are learning English, substitution provides a simple way of deploying new vocabulary within sentences.

Usually, places, characters and names are substituted. One word of warning though – some children are tempted to substitute too much and then find that they cannot recall all the changes so the plot ... literally ... falls apart! It may be worth limiting or staging the substitutions so that you gain success. Model how to change a story by redrawing or changing the class map and using this for telling of the new version.

So, a simple substitution for the 'Billy Goats Gruff' might start like this:

One upon a time there were three shaggy sheep who lived beside a stream ...

2. Additions

In some ways making additions comes quite naturally. Children retelling a story will often start adding extra bits in the same way that in conversation when they are telling about things that have happened, they may embellish for an audience ... so the tale grows in the telling ...

The simplest way to move into addition is by adding in more description, e.g.

One upon a time there were three shaggy old sheep who lived beside a deep stream ...

You could build on this by:

- adding in more dialogue;
- adding in a new character;

Changing stories

Perhaps an otter tries to persuade the troll to stop acting so unreasonably!

- adding in new incidents –

The troll is afraid of the sheep and sends for help!

Usually, you will find that you are not only adding extra events or description but also substituting as well. Keep demonstrating how to add and embellish.

3. Alterations

Of course, a substitution is a form of alteration. However, most simple substitutions have little consequence. By 'alteration' I mean a change that is significant and changes the direction of the tale – alterations have a knock on effect!

It is worth beginning by just making changes within the story – so that the children have the overall comfort of the original, to act as a large writing frame and provide a structure within which they can manoeuvre. You could try altering:

- the nature of one or more of the characters, e.g. the troll is afraid of the goats;
- settings, e.g. put Goldilocks onto a modern estate;

Many teachers like to alter the ending of the story – because children find endings difficult. Thinking up new ways to end the story, twisting the tale in a different direction helps to build up a store of possibilities for the children to draw upon when they are creating. So teachers often focus upon:

- altering the way the story opens or ends;

Another common approach is to alter a key event within the tale or add in some new ones as a result. I remember hearing a year two girl retelling the gingerbread man in which the man got seized by a hungry girl called Gretel and eaten up! It was a lovely example of one tale wandering into another but did rather surprise all the characters who were chasing the gingerbread man! So you can also:

- alter key events within the story.

4. Change of viewpoint

This is far more sophisticated than a basic retelling with additions and changes. The children have to see the story from another angle. Plenty of drama and lots of modelling by the teacher can help the children into changes of viewpoint. There are two key ways to do this:

- retell a tale from the viewpoint of another character;
- retell a tale as a different text type, e.g. as a diary entry, letter or news report.

Changing stories

Seeing things from a different viewpoint is enhanced by activities such as hot seating. The teacher writing in role or talking in role about what has happened also helps. Providing opportunities for role-play will also allow the children to step into different roles.

Re-cycle the basic plot

Finally, we come to the idea of just re-using the underlying pattern, plot or theme and totally rewriting the story. So, 'the Gingerbread Man' is a story about a wrong doer who is chased but meets a well-deserved end! 'The Billy Goats Gruff' is a journey story in which there is a barrier to overcome. Or 'Goldilocks' is a tale about someone who enters a forbidden place and breaks, ruins or steals something of value only to be faced with the 'owner' or guardian!

Re-using the basic plot means that you can start with a traditional tale but reset it as a science fiction, detective or any other genre. The original tale just provides the plot pattern and theme.

Moving the telling into writing

Do not consider asking the children to write until they have a story to tell. Many may fail if you ask them to create a story on the hoof as they write ... thorough preparation will provide success – progress and motivation. Everyone will start with an oral substitution – some may proceed further. Let's see if we can map out a rough idea of how the storymaking process will run – bearing in mind that there may well be variations that you discover work.

Story Innovation Process

1. Tell the new story with actions.
2. Draw a new story map or storyboard.

3. Retell the story daily – with the pupils increasingly joining in while the teacher gradually withdraws.

4. Move onto story circles and pairs as well as whole class.
5. Once the children have internalised the story into their long-term working memory – begin innovation.
6. Teacher models an innovation and creates a new story map/storyboard.
7. The teacher demonstrates how to use this to retell the new version.

8. Class and teacher retell new version.

9. Teacher leads the children through creating their innovation.
10. Children draw their new map and retell their innovation.

11. Teacher demonstrates shared writing of class innovation.
10. Pupils write or record their own innovations.
12. Polishing and publishing of stories.

This process allows for success. The children only move on to the writing when they really do have something to say. Often when children are asked to write, they struggle because there is too much happening inside their minds. They have to orchestrate too many things – the pencil grip, spellings, where does the dot go ... let alone what to say. If some of the writing processes are not easy and automatic, the brain is overloaded and there is insufficient cognitive space for composition. Weaker writers will worry about handwriting and spelling and this intervenes and cuts out the ability to compose – indeed, it just makes writing laborious, painful and dull. No wonder so many start fidgeting and fooling about!

However, if when you sit down to write you really have a story to tell then the child is not only more motivated to write but also will find it easier because it has released a large chunk of cognitive space.

Now this all sounds well and good but ... we have been putting a lot of effort into developing the compositional side of writing – what about the transcriptional skills? These too need attention and developing.

- Handwriting – lots of work on fine and gross motor skills leading into regular handwriting practice – for young children this may be daily.
- Spelling – daily phonics and spelling work;
- Sentences – daily sentence games to develop the ability to compose and manipulate sentences.

With some children you may just be delighted that they can tell a story and at this moment that is sufficient – because you know that if they are asked to write it down, they will fail (having said that, I have seen many examples of strugglers so motivated that they have been more prepared to put pencil to paper). It may be worth recording children so that you can demonstrate progress. Do this right at the start before they have really learned a story – and then the transcript can be used to identify progress after a term.

Practising spellings

A very strong foundation in phonics will pay off in early writing. The ability to segment words into their constituent sounds – or hear a word clearly so that it can be spelled is fundamental. This is supported by knowing which letter, or letters, might represent different sounds. Finally, plenty of practice in writing the letters down will reap rewards because spelling liberates writing.

Phonics needs to be daily, systematic and applied into reading and writing. It works best through daily whole class teaching and in the initial stages through children having at least two group sessions a week where they run through:

- Writing/reading sounds;
- Writing/reading cvc words;
- Writing/reading tricky words;
- Writing/reading sentences;
- Blending and segmenting games.

The teacher dictates the sounds, word and sentences on the back of what has been taught – so the children are revisiting and applying what has been taught. It is this very focused practice that helps to liberate writing – so the children begin to make the link and see how it can enable them to compose and communicate.

There are enough phonic games and activities that have become part of the literacy strategy's support materials to last any teacher a lifetime. However, as the children move into spelling many schools have found that an effective way to improve spelling is through daily practise using letter fans and mini whiteboards. This works well in year 2 but also pays dividends in year 1 – and some of the games can be used with reception children.

Spelling games:

Again, if you want children to become swifter spellers then you will need to play spelling games on a daily basis. If you organise the handing out of mini whiteboards effectively this should only take ten minutes or so. But remember – it is the constant repetition, embedding the patterns in the brain that makes the difference. When discussing spelling use a problem solving approach. For instance, get the children discussing errors and thinking about different ways to remember key words. For example, write up the common error 'whent' and ask the children to explain the muddle and think of ways to recall how to spell 'when' and 'went'.

Whilst phonics is the key strategy for early spelling, use a multi-sensory approach for remembering spellings. Try using colours to make difficult parts stand out in a word. Try chanting common tricky words and patterns. Try using actions to help recall common errors.

Finally, what spellings need to be learned? It is essential that you have a systematic approach to phonics. It is also important to use assessment so that you know exactly what to teach to which groups. Once the basic programme has been established and you begin to move into spelling, you can be guided by:

1. The children's common errors – especially common words and patterns that they keep getting wrong and often need.
2. Words from the most common word list.
3. Words needed for the text type – this is crucial. If you are writing a story in year 1, the chances are that the children will need the word 'once'. Therefore this needs to be taught or at least provided on a story 'spelling card'.

Right at the start of the storymaking process the teacher needs to identify the key spellings that will ultimately be needed to write the story or an innovation of the story. These words need to be practised daily so that when the children come to write, the act of writing is easier – they have been well prepared. Anyway, here are the main games – though you will also have others that may be handy.

• *Is it right?*

Write up three variations of a word on the board (wos woz was) – and ask the children to write down the correct one. Then discuss – how do you know – how do you remember? Feed off their common muddles and errors.

• *See it and chant it*

Begin by discussing the spelling and 'looking' carefully at it. Take a mental snapshot and try to see it in your mind. The visual part of the brain is in the top left hand corner so they can raise their eyes upwards and to the left to try and see it.

This is also a whole class variation of 'look, say, cover, write, check'. The main difference is that instead of 'say', which seems a bit tame to me, it is more effective if you CHANT the spelling rhythmically – preferably with actions. It will be more likely to stick in the brain with rhythm and action. Anyway, you chant and then cover the word. The children have a go at writing it on their board. Remind them to listen to the chant in their heads – can they 'see' the word? Before they show you their efforts ask them to look at what they have written and if it doesn't look right then they should change it ... or at least underline the part of the word that is causing a problem so that you can see where they are uncertain.

• *Speedy spelling*

This game relies on kinesthetic learning. Write up a tricky common word or a word with a common pattern within it. Everyone copies this down (ideally in 'joined' writing) and then double checks their neighbour has copied correctly. The game is to write the word as many times as possible with accurate spelling in say thirty seconds. Encourage them to chant the spelling as they write.

• Gaps

This is a simple game. All you do is miss out letters. It could be fairly limited (th-y) or fairly open (s - - -p).

• Countdown

In memory of the blessed Richard Whitely – choose two vowels and five consonants – how many words can be made?

• Riddles

In this game you provide clues. For instance, you might be working on words that have double consonants (*muddle*). You give several clues, e.g. *I'm thinking of a word that in America they call 'trash'. Some people say 'you're a load of old ' ....', also – we throw it in the bin ... and it has a double consonant in the middle.* (Hopefully, they will write 'rubbish' and not 'rubish').

• Common patterns

It is worth endlessly returning to the most common starts, middles and ends – especially, 'ly', 'ing', 'ed'. This could be simple dictation. So on Monday you might dictate words like 'jump' (add on 'ing'). On Tuesday you might dictate words like 'move' (cross out the 'e' and add on 'ing' – 'moving'). On Wednesday you might dictate words like 'run (double – 'running') ... on Thursday mix them all up and on Friday – have a mini test!

• Shannon's game

This game is the same as hangman (though drawing a clown's face might be more acceptable!). The difference is that the children have to guess the letters in order – this means that they have to consider the serial probability – what letter could/could not occur next.

• Daily – segment and blend

I think that it would be worth having several minutes a day where the children rapidly segment and blend. This could be oral with an action just to practise the ability to say a word and segment it ... or they could draw a mini phoneme frame to spell the sounds into:

f	i	sh

Changing stories

• *Find a Rhyme*

This is an easy game that leads neatly into discussing which spelling patterns are most likely. Write a word on the board and the children have half a minute to write rhyming words. Try using –

pain, feel, phone, might, tries, rope, weed, pail, boat, dream, pace, drive, foal, fake, book, bar, lock, sack, out, good, bed, sad, boy, say, late, tree, fly, glow, shoe, fame, slave, mine, soon, tool, toast, greet, rap, smash, sat, pay, nest, pill, sit, mine, sing, link, slip, got, hop, lump, poke, bug.

• *A final thought on spelling*

Of course, spelling is for writing. Many children can get a spelling right when all they have to do is focus upon one word but in the hurly burly of composition the brain may be elsewhere. It is helpful if you can refer to spelling during the course of shared writing – however, this needs to be quick reminders so that pace and flow is not lost.

Practising sentences

In the same way that right at the start of the storymaking process the teacher needs to identify the key spellings that will ultimately be needed to write the story or an innovation of the story, we also need to think about the sorts of sentences that will be needed.

These sentences need to be practised daily so that when the children come to write, the act of writing will be easier – they have been well prepared. This may mean practising 'suddenly' sentences, 'once upon a time' sentences and so on. In particular, it is worth practising making up sentences using different connectives.

If children have not heard how a connective is used in a sentence then there is no chance that they will somehow be able to magically do this on their own. They need plenty of practise 'hearing' how a complex sentence works and then 'saying' them ... as well as reading and writing them. But the 'hearing' and 'saying' must come first.

Certain stories will throw up obvious sentence types to rehearse. But also consider what will help the children make progress – in year two, they will need to begin varying sentences, handling compound and complex sentences, using a variety of connectives, varying openings, using interesting vocabulary ... and all this needs daily practice.

If the children are uncertain then you will need to model orally and then in writing – demonstrating and then asking for contributions. Once they become confident, you can move to writing on the whiteboards.

The really cunning teacher picks up on the spellings that have been practising and then reuses these in the sentences being written. And then in shared writing the spellings and sentences are used within the composition ... and the children are expected to use these in their own writing! If you look in the appendix, you will find the 'language bank' that identifies key aspects of language such as connectives to teach each year. These are embedded into the stories being learned but will also need regular practice.

Try beginning sessions with spelling games, followed by sentences. This will need to be well organised, otherwise you will eat into the main body of the session. Most of the games can be done orally, though with more confident writers you will want to use mini whiteboards. Some of the games lend themselves to using words and parts of sentences on strips of card to make the game more tactile and visual – rather like a maths washing line. You could also use an interactive whiteboard. Anyway, here are the main games – though you will also have others that may be handy.

• *My Copycat*

This game is handy for the youngest and least confident. Stick your hand up a glove puppet – which then says a sentence. The children have to LISTEN and REPEAT. The puppet can say sentences in different ways – loud, soft, slowly, quickly, bro-ken in-to syll-a-bles, musically. You can say different types of sentences and increase to three or four at a go – or simple rhymes or mini tales. Remember that many children enter school and have yet still to say a complete sentence as they are at the stage of one or two words representing whole sentences.

As the children grow in confidence, move on to 'innovation', so the glove puppet says a sentence and the children use the stem to invent their own. The puppet might say, 'in the picture I can see an old man sitting on the ground'. Then the children turn to their partner and use the stem 'in the picture I can see ...' to create a new sentence.

• *Sentence Builder*

In this game you give the children one word (*dog*) and the children have to make up a sentence using that word (*I saw an old dog running along*). Once they are confident with this, move to two words (*cat/jumped – the angry cat jumped onto the table*). In the end you might get as far as three words and introduce using connectives (*dog barked because – the dog barked because the cat stole its bone*).

If the children cannot rapidly make up a sentence then they will not be able to write whole texts so this is an important skill. Try it orally and in writing. When inventing sentences orally ask the children to put in the punctuation using an action and sound. This shows you that they know that there should be a full stop and it acts as a really good learning device to remind them. Be ruthless on insisting on full stops orally and in writing right from the start – get those footballs in!

Changing stories

• *Boring sentences*

In this game you write up a really dull sentence (or paragraph for the more confident) and the children have to 'improve' it. This could be done in various ways. Take the sentence.

The dog went down the road.

This doesn't actually build a very powerful picture in the reader's mind and could be improved. You could:

1. Change words – *The Alsatian limped down the High Street.*
2. Add words in – *The shaggy dog went carefully down the deserted road.*
3. Add words on – *The dog went down the road because the cat had bitten its tail.*

Remember the following:

■ watch out for weak nouns as well as verbs ('Ostrich' not just 'bird');
■ don't just add in adjectives – collect a bag of adverbs and get using them;
■ add on by using a connective at the end of the sentence and for mature writers get them adding on at the start (*Because the pet shop had been broken into, the dog went down the road ...*).

It is worth also introducing children to using:

■ alliteration – repeating a sound close together – *Sam the serious seal ate cereal slowly ... ;*
■ simile using 'like' – *broccoli is like moss;*
■ simile using 'as' – *as thin as an eyelash.*

• *Sentence Doctor*

This game is about spotting mistakes. Feed off the children's common errors so that they get used to spotting the sort of thing that they often get wrong – then they can move on to simple response partnering and looking for their own errors as well as places to improve. Write up sentences that have mistakes – spellings, missing words, punctuation errors, shifts in tenses, incorrect use of pronouns, etc.

• *Finish it off!*

Provide part of a sentence for the children to complete. Try using openings, endings and then middles (which is quite hard!).

• *Drop in*

This can become a simple part of the children's 'polishing' (editing) routine – where they get used to re-reading their work to find places where they can 'drop in' words.

Changing stories

The game is to provide them with a sentence and they drop in words. Remember to encourage adverbs as well as adjectives. Also – watch out for the overuse of adjectives as this can make the writing worse!

You could try a game called 'shorten' – which involves giving the children an over-written sentence to shorten – or play a game called 'lengthen' in which you give them a very short sentence that they have to make longer!

• *Join it*

This is a very important game and worth playing in year two on many occasions. The idea is to provide the children with two short simple sentences that relate to each other chronologically. The children then have to join them using a connective (not 'and' or 'then' – because we know the children can use those two!).

The door opened.
The princess came out.

Now the children have to make one sentence by using a connective either between the sentences or at the front, e.g.

As the door opened, the princess came out.
The door opened as the princess came out.

Words that would work well here include:

As, as soon as, after, before, although, immediately, when, whenever, while, so, because, but.

• *Imitation*

In this game you simply model a type of sentence that you want the children to use and then they have to innovate on the pattern. For instance, you might show year 2 children how to do an adverb starter (*Slowly, she crept along*) and then use a bag of adverbs to invent their own 'adverb starters'.

• *Punctuating stories*

Getting into the habit of putting in a full stop can be very hard. After all, when we speak and read punctuation does not make a sound. It does very little that is memorable. If you have many children who find this a challenge, a simple but effective tactic is to introduce 'sound punctuation' in year one. Perhaps during the second term where the writing is beginning to flow, learn several stories in the normal way but for every punctuation mark add in a sound effect and action. This makes great fun and also more importantly, it makes the punctuation memorable. You will see that when they write the story down, they are more likely to use punctuation. Have a go at this – it works like magic! Also try a game where you read sentences and put in the sounds and actions for the punctuation.

• *Final thoughts on sentences*

For many children talking and writing in whole sentences does not come easily because they have not had sufficient experience of hearing and saying sentences. It is vital that this is addressed in a vigorous and focussed manner because if the brain does not acquire sentence patterns early on, it can become too late and in extreme cases of deprivation there are children who will never be able to acquire syntax. Sentence acquisition comes through modelling, reflecting and extending children's responses – and plenty of reading, composing, playing and talking.

Modelling writing

In the same way that children can learn a story orally through imitation so too children can learn how to write by imitation. It has always intrigued me that teachers are quite happy to stick up a big book in reception and start the business of reading together from early on but are reluctant to write in front of children. Every opportunity should be taken to model writing. We have to show children how to plan, write and then edit or polish their writing – making simple improvements and ensuring accuracy.

Certainly, before the children write their story down (if they are to) then the teacher will be writing up the class innovation in front of the children. This is a key strategy for drawing upon all sorts of aspects of teaching – handwriting, spelling, and punctuation through to using good words. When the teacher is 'modelling' or 'demonstrating', it is worth trying to provide a 'running commentary', explaining what you are doing. For instance, it is important to demonstrate how to:

- say the sentence to yourself (rehearsal);
- write it down;
- reread what you have written.

Re-reading is important. Firstly, because you need to check that you have written what you intended to write. Secondly, it provides the link into making up the next sentence. Finally, more mature writers might think of a way of improving or 'polishing' what has been written – by adding in or changing words for instance. Make it obvious when you are referring to word lists or using specific words or sentences that you have been practising. In the main, 'modelling' or 'demonstration' is used to show children:

- new things, e.g. a new text type;
- hard things, e.g. dialogue;
- progress – things that if the children use them, they will make progress, e.g. using a variety of connectives.

Changing stories

When you are setting about modelling, it is important to be clear what it is that you will specifically be demonstrating – the aspect of progress that you are emphasising or teaching.

Shared writing

Shared writing is when the children are joining in – the truth is that very often some of the time you are deciding what happens but also young children will want to make suggestions. Keep challenging and also maintain the pace. I have seen some miserably slow writing sessions where we have ended up with several sentences up on the board after having spent a lot of time sounding each word out. Then the children went off and wrote several pages! It's a shame if the teacher cannot write as well as the children!

What you end up with on the board needs to be just above where the majority of the children are. If most are at about level two – then you need to show them level three!

It is also worth writing up whole stories and not just openings. Children need to see every aspect of a story modelled. Many teachers in year two spread a story out over a week so that the children see a new part of the story modelled daily.

Writing journals

Writing journals are very handy as a resource for children and could be used probably from year 1 onwards – certainly in year 2. The journals contain all the useful reminders and lists and models that we use with the children. It might contain things like 'words to use instead of 'said' as well as story maps, spelling lists for specific stories or pieces of non-fiction. For instance, under 'recounts' there might be a handy list of connectives such as 'first, next, after that, later on, finally'.

In Stella's year 2 class on the Isle of Wight, she uses green folders for their journals. These are now used across the school and the folder will move up with the children each year, to be developed and added to. When I visited the school, the children were writing and it was interesting to see how different children used different pages. One girl used her 'adjectives' page whilst one lad was using 'adverbs'. He told me that his favourite word was 'majestically'!

Interestingly, many of the pages in the folders were lists that the children had created, gathering words and examples for themselves. This sense of ownership seems to be important in securing usage of the journals. They need to be the children's own writing thesaurus. Here is a list of what Stella has in their folders at the moment:

- story toolkits, e.g. Billy Goats Gruff
- adverbs/my adverbs
- openers
- extra openers

Changing stories

- fairy tale characters
- fairy tale settings
- fairy tale master toolkit
- my ambitious adjectives
- powerful verbs
- where – prepositions
- punctuation pyramid
- question words
- said toolkit
- useful openers y2
- useful openers y3/4

Chapter 3 Making up stories

The third aspect of storymaking is children making up stories on their own (often known as 'invention'). Of course, to do this they have to draw upon their bank of stories as well as their general experience of life, things that have happened to them, stories read and seen as well as new ideas that they think of for themselves – new possibilities.

It is quite possible to involve very young children in inventing stories. After all, many children chatter away to themselves as they play, telling the story of what they are doing. Storymaking is a form of play and inventing a tale together can be easy, fun to do and become a natural part of classroom life.

To encourage children to make up and play at stories, many children just need the provision of dressing up clothes, toys, sand, water, cardboard boxes, special role play areas ... and they are away. There is a strong tradition in infant classes of this sort of provision.

The specific phase of 'invention' can be moved into as the children build up a bank of known narratives – certainly once several stories have been learned you can begin to successfully make stories up together because already fundamental patterns – 'story pathways' – have been paid down in the brain.

For younger pupils, you might consider holding regular weekly story inventing sessions. Having said that, I do know of reception classes where story inventing is a daily part of what the children do.

You could invent stories with the whole class, groups, pairs or individuals. The basic approach is to make up a story orally – initially without the fuss of writing it down. The teacher guides the process – though over time it is important that the children become increasingly involved and independent until in the end they can invent stories for themselves. This means that the teacher has to 'withdraw' from dominating and shaping the story invention sessions.

When inventing a new story, it is useful to reuse familiar characters, settings, events and patterns as well as encouraging new ideas. Keep reusing connectives, sentences and story patterns to help link ideas together and provide underlying structures for their creations. For instance – once the teacher is armed with a simple set of connectives then a story becomes possible –

Once upon a time ...
One day ...
Unfortunately ...
Luckily ...
Finally ...

All this should ideally appear seamless and natural to the children with the teacher lending a guiding hand.

Making up stories

Starting Points

It is worth experimenting and building up a range of different strategies to encourage the invention of stories. Here are some possibilities:

- making up another story about a favourite character from a story or picture book;
- make up a story about a puppet or toy;
- reuse a familiar plot pattern;
- hide items in a box or bag for a character to find;
- use a set of character and settings cards to choose 'who' and 'where';
- give the 'baddie' a negative characteristic – sad, lonely, angry, mean, spiteful, foolish, cunning, sly … ;
- give the main character a characteristic – clever, brave, hungry, lonely, hopeful, careful, kind, generous, happy …;
- use a set of dilemma cards to choose something that goes wrong;
- take a simple picture book like 'Pig in the Pond' or 'Owl Babies' and retell in new setting with new characters;
- Turn a nursery rhyme into a story – 'Humpty Dumpty', 'Sing a song of sixpence', 'Lucy locket', '3 Blind Mice', 'Little Jack Horner', 'Jack Spratt', 'Simple Simon', 'Mary's Lamb', 'Hey diddle diddle', 'Goosey Goosey Gander', 'Little Miss Muffet'.
- Choose a basic theme for the story, e.g.
  a. Helping someone
  b. Mistaken identity
  c. Feeling afraid
  d. Surprises
  e. Getting in trouble
  f. Sad – happy
  g. Alone – friendship
  h. Wrong – right
  i. Silly – wise
  j. Mean – generous
- Music played – time to day dream, to close your eyes and begin to 'see' a story;
- Pictures to observe – what happened before, during and next;
- Posters of paintings with something happening;
- Video clips or stills;
- Writing extra incidents around a known tale;
- Objects or puppets in a story bag or box;
- Intriguing objects – a shiny button, a lantern, an old map, a key;
- Places – inventing on location – what happened here?
- Teacher in role – telling their story;
- A letter arrives, half a secret message is discovered;
- Drama – acting out and creating a story together;

Making up stories

- Using felt figures or puppets or toys;
- Drawing a large story map to use for inventions.

Whole class inventions

Remember that when you are making up stories with young children, you do not need anything complicated – KEEP IT SIMPLE. Try to avoid inventing a rambling, complex tale that does not act as a simple model for the children.

Settle the children down and introduce the stimulus or starting point. Then just scaffold their ideas as the tale unfolds:

'Once upon a time there was – shall we have a girl, boy or maybe an animal this time? – a fox! – ok – let's start again – Once upon a time there was a fox called – what should we call the fox? – Kirk! – Once upon a time there was a fox called Kirk who lived ... now where did he live ...?'

In your mind keep a simple story frame to guide the story and it will give you confidence:

- Introduce a character in a setting – *'once upon a time there was ... who lived ...'*
- Get them doing something or going somewhere – *'one day ...'*
- Something goes wrong – *'unfortunately ...'*
- Sort it out – *'luckily ...'*
- Have a good ending – *'happily ever after'.*

The basic plots

The more that I have discussed stories with teachers and children, the more we have come to realise that there are a number of underlying patterns that seem to be repeated endlessly in all sorts of variations and blends. Christopher Hampton categorises seven basic plots including tragedy. There seems to me to be a few basic patterns that are worth knowing about as simple stories can be built around these ideas.

1. Problem/resolution
This is the basic pattern – everything is all right, there is a problem and it gets sorted out.

2. Beating the monster.
In some senses, this is the same pattern. Remember that monsters, ogres and dragons are all metaphors for anything bad in our lives. In this tale – everything is all right; a monster arrives and has to be overcome – often by the weakest person. The monster could be an ogre, a savage dog, bullies, a nasty teacher, disease or unemployment.

3. Warning
This is a very handy version of the above two plots. You begin with a warning such as 'do not play near the canal'. Of course, the main characters do whatever it is that they are not supposed to do – and get into trouble, need a rescue and have learned a lesson by the end.

4. Quest

This is another very common pattern. In it a character is given a task and has to make a journey to complete it. From 'Lord of the Rings' to 'Red Riding Hood', literature is full of journey stories.

5. Wishing/barriers

Many stories involve a character who really wants something but is stopped by a barrier – in the end the barrier is overcome and often the main character attains their heart's desire but it is often not worth having! Life is all about overcoming barriers from trolls who block the way to wicked emperors.

6. Lost/found/chased

In 'lost' stories either the character gets lost or loses something precious. In a 'finding' story the finding of something significant leads into the tale – from corn to magic brushes! In a chase, a character is pursued.

7. Cinderella

This is the most common pattern around the world. It is the tale of someone oppressed who through diligence, kindness or loyalty manages to win through – sometimes with the assistance of a 'helper'. I suppose the little red hen is a form of Cinderella – though she gets there on her own!

8. Magical powers

In these tales some form of magical power or trick is involved in the story.

9. Character flaw

Character flaw stories are about characters that through some flaw find themselves in trouble. Often by the end they have learned a lesson or changed.

10. Fables/myths/legends/family stories

These types have their own patterns – many of which can be imitated and innovated upon or borrowed to create new tales. Family stories (recounts from children's own lives), for instance, are especially helpful as they can be fictionalised as if they happened to someone else and turned into a story.

Tell it – draw it – retell it

When children are working independently, it can help if they get used to preparing their story in two ways:

1. Deciding what will happen – talking the ideas through and drawing a map, storyboard or mountain to capture their ideas.
2. Telling the story and retelling it – turning the decisions into story language.

The teacher has to model this – deciding, telling, drawing, retelling and so on.

Making up stories

Record or Write it

Now it may well be that you are just going to make a story up for the fun of it – and it will never be recorded in any way. However, there are various possibilities for recording inventions:

1. Children retell their story to another class;
2. Tape or record the story;
3. Video – use a digital blue camera;
4. Draw the story map and annotate;
5. Draw the main events onto a story board;
6. Map the main events onto a story mountain;
7. Draw or write notes on the main events into a flow chart – which provides a simple paragraph planner;
8. Write the story up as it develops onto a flip chart or blank big book.

A few thoughts on character

Characterisation is not easy for young children. In the main their characters move through the stories with events happening to them – rather than the characters causing events. One simple way to introduce the idea of characterisation is to provide a menu of 'feelings' to choose from. These might be positive or negative feeling, e.g.

Kind	Sad
Generous	Lonely
Happy	Angry
Brave	Spiteful
Clever	Greedy
Excited	Cruel

Incidentally, it can be fun to have lists of characters, settings or feelings or dilemmas in sets of six – and use a dice to select randomly. Anyway, as soon as you say *'Once upon a time there was a foolish fox who ...'*, the possibility of something interesting occurs. The fox is foolish so what silly thing might happen? Deciding on an emotion leads you into thinking about how a character's disposition will influence events – what the character might 'say or do'. Genuine characterisation is shown through action and dialogue.

Furthermore, if a character is lonely at the start of the story – by the end they may well have found a friend and be happy! In this way, simple character development can be achieved.

Character description should be kept to a minimum as it can interfere with the story. Try bringing a character on with a descriptive 'sentence of three', e.g. *He wore a red cloak, pointed shoes and a tall hat.*

Making up stories

Other tips on characterisation are:

- Do not have too many characters – one or two will do;
- Choose a good name for your characters;
- Try re-using the same character in different stories so you get to know her/him well;
- Build up a bank of stock characters to call upon;
- Use a menu of 'feelings';
- Think about or act out what a character might say or do.

A few thoughts on dialogue

Dialogue is hard. It needs to be modelled many times – and practised many times. Begin by using a new line when someone speaks. Then move onto speech bubbles. Then pop the bubble and leave the speech marks.

Provide simple reminders on the wall and on story cards to show the children how to set out dialogue. Avoid stories that have lots of dialogue in them. Collect powerful speech verbs on the wall, story cards or in their writing journal – and make sure they use them! Introduce in year 2, the adverb – *he muttered <u>mysteriously</u>*.

When writing dialogue, ask the children to think about what this character might say (remind them about the character's 'feeling').

A few thoughts on settings

Use setting cards to provide a simple bank to call upon. Use the digital camera to take photos of local places that can be added to the bank of settings. To describe settings can be simple, if you show the setting through the character's eyes – what they saw:

Shamila looked at the dark forest. The trees were taller than a house and in between them strange shadows flickered!

Have a wall chart or page of 'settings' words to support the children when writing. The children only need one or two details to build the picture for the reader and then they can get on with the rest of the story.

A few thoughts on endings

The ending is crucial. I like to separate the end from the resolution – the resolution sorts out whatever has gone wrong – the ending is reserved for showing the reader how the main character has changed or what they have learned. It can help to take the main character home – and mentioning that they all lived 'happily ever after'!

Chapter 4 Using the bank of stories

There are six stories for reception, year 1 and year 2. Certainly in reception and year 1 you will want to tell and learn more than this. Each story is accompanied by a spelling card. This has spaces for spellings that the children can add for their innovations (The presence of spellings in reception does not mean that they should be writing whole stories – some teachers in year 1 may be dipping back and find the cards handy – in the main in reception the stories are oral). Also there is a list of suggested activities – and some ideas for innovations. In the appendices I have shown one extra 'journey' story (with a warning) that would be good for any year group + a story map so that you can see what one looks like. Keep your maps simple and clear – with a pathway that shows the route through the story. Add in a few connectives or prompt words if need be and use colour to make hard bits memorable.

Some teachers fight shy of stories such as 'The Hobyahs'. Actually, what may appear quite gory to us is often very popular with children and the fact that at the end the Hobyahs are seen off is a comfort – such stories may well help children cope with their fears. Good does triumph.

If you look carefully, you will see the various language features such as connectives built into the stories – try to emphasise these and provide an action as these are the aspects that you want the children to learn. The language bank and action bank are in the appendices – with a plan.

If you find the way in which I have written the stories makes it hard for you to say them fluently and rhythmically then please do adapt and alter. I have left the objectives blank in the plan (appendices) because the new strategy objectives are due in September 2006. What we do know is that storytelling will appear across the primary years.

Good luck – and have fun! You are passing on a culture and creating lasting metaphors in children's minds. These stories will become beacons in the dark night – in eighty years from now these tales will still be alive inside the children's minds. You are passing on something lasting and of the most infinite mystery to do with the human spirit and how we cherish it within ourselves and within the children we teach and learn with.

Pie Corbett
July 2006

The Little Red Hen

Once upon a time there was a little red hen who lived on a farm.
Early one morning she woke up and went outside. There she found some corn.

'Who will help me plant the corn?' said the little red hen.

'Not I,' said the bull.
'Not I,' said the cat.
'Not I,' said the rat.
'Oh very well, I'll do it myself,' said the little red hen –
and so she did!

'Who will help me water the corn?' said the little red hen.

'Not I,' said the bull.
'Not I,' said the cat.
'Not I,' said the rat.
'Oh very well, I'll do it myself,' said the little red hen –
and so she did!

'Who will help me cut the corn?' said the little red hen.

'Not I,' said the bull.
'Not I,' said the cat.
'Not I,' said the rat.
'Oh very well, I'll do it myself,' said the little red hen –
and so she did!

'Who will help me carry the corn to the mill?' said the little red hen.

'Not I,' said the bull.
'Not I,' said the cat.
'Not I,' said the rat.
'Oh very well, I'll do it myself,' said the little red hen –
and so she did!

'Who will help me grind the corn?' said the little red hen.

'Not I,' said the bull.
'Not I,' said the cat.
'Not I,' said the rat.
'Oh very well, I'll do it myself,' said the little red hen –
and so she did!

'Who will help me knead the bread?' said the little red hen.

'Not I,' said the bull.
'Not I,' said the cat.
'Not I,' said the rat.
'Oh very well, I'll do it myself,' said the little red hen –
and so she did!

'Who will help me bake the bread?' said the little red hen.

'Not I,' said the bull.
'Not I,' said the cat.
'Not I,' said the rat.
'Oh very well, I'll do it myself,' said the little red hen –
and so she did!

'Who will help me eat the bread?' said the little red hen.

'I will,' said the bull.
'I will,' said the cat.
'I will,' said the rat.
'Oh no you won't,' said the little red hen, 'I'll eat it myself –
and so she did!

Little Red Hen Story Card

Once upon a time
was
little
who
farm
early one morning
woke
outside
There
found
eat
myself
so

bull
cat
rat

Little Red Hen – ideas and innovations.

Ideas

- Farm animals.
- Raising chicks from eggs.
- How animals are looked after.
- Farm collage.
- Read Farmer Duck by Martin Waddell.
- Old MacDonald had a farm.
- Tractors and farm machinery and tools.
- What are farms for?
- Corn – growing seeds.
- Bread making – recipes.
- Being selfish – helping others.
- If everyone helps it's quicker and easier!
- Hot seat the little red hen.
- Act the story out.

Innovations

This is a good story to start with as it is easy to learn – but remember do not rush into innovations until you are certain that the children can retell the tale independently. This is ideal for simple substitution – just change the hard working hen for another creature and alter the three animals that will not help, e.g.

Once upon a time there was a little white goose who lived on a farm.
Early one morning she woke up and went outside. There she found some corn.

'Who will help me plant the corn?' said the little white goose.

'Not I,' said the horse.
'Not I,' said the sheep.
'Not I,' said the goat.
'Oh very well, I'll do it myself,' said the little white goose –
and so she did!

The Gingerbread Man

Once not twice but upon a time there was a little old woman who baked a gingerbread man. Unfortunately the gingerbread man ran out of the house!

'Stop, stop little gingerbread man,' shouted the little old woman.

But the gingerbread man shouted, 'Run, run as fast as you can, you can't catch me I'm the gingerbread man.'

So the little old lady chased the gingerbread man down the lane till he came to the horse's field.

'Stop, stop little gingerbread man,' shouted the horse.

But the gingerbread man shouted, 'Run, run as fast as you can, you can't catch me I'm the gingerbread man.'

So the little old lady and the horse chased the gingerbread man across the field till he came to the old cow.

'Stop, stop little gingerbread man,' shouted the old cow.

But the gingerbread man shouted, 'Run, run as fast as you can, you can't catch me I'm the gingerbread man.'

So the little old lady, the horse and the old cow chased the gingerbread man down the lane till he came to the goat's field.

'Stop, stop little gingerbread man,' shouted the cow.

But the gingerbread man shouted, 'Run, run as fast as you can, you can't catch me I'm the gingerbread man.'

So the little old lady, the horse, the cow and the goat chased the gingerbread man down the lane till he came to a sleepy dog.

'Stop, stop little gingerbread man,' shouted the sleepy dog.

But the gingerbread man shouted, 'Run, run as fast as you can, you can't catch me I'm the gingerbread man.'

So the little old lady, the horse, the cow, the goat and the sleepy dog chased the gingerbread man down the lane.

Finally, he came to a stream where he met a fox, a lean fox, a mean fox.

'Quick, quick little gingerbread man – climb onto my tail.'

So the gingerbread man climbed onto his tail.

'My feet are getting all wet,' moaned the gingerbread man.

'Quick, quick little gingerbread man – climb onto my back.'

So the gingerbread man climbed onto his back.

'My legs are getting all wet,' moaned the gingerbread man.

'Quick, quick little gingerbread man – climb onto my head.'

So the gingerbread man climbed onto his head.

'My hands are getting all wet,' moaned the gingerbread man.

'Quick, quick little gingerbread man – climb onto my ears.'

So the gingerbread man climbed onto his ears.

'My head is getting all wet,' moaned the gingerbread man.

'Quick, quick little gingerbread man – jump onto my nose.'

So the gingerbread man jumped onto his nose.

Unfortunately, the fox ate him up – in – one – big – gulp!

The Gingerbread Man Story Card

Once upon a time
there
was
who
gingerbread
out
down
across
shouted
chased
can't
chased
but
so
fox
stream
moaned
climbed
unfortunately

The Gingerbread Man – ideas and innovations

Ideas
- Baking gingerbread.
- Other cooking.
- Recipes.
- Designing gingerbread men.
- Cutting out men shapes – Decorating shapes.
- Farm animals.
- Draw the path the man took – making maps of journeys and walks.
- Foxes – where they live/eat.
- Preposition games – hiding a doll in relation to a box (above, below inside, etc).
- Hot seat characters about what they saw!

Innovations

Another simple tale – my guess is that it will take about two weeks of daily telling to get to know it well enough to move on to a class innovation. This is ideal for simple substitution – change the man into something else – what else could you bake, e.g. a gingerbread mouse. Alter who cooks the mouse and the places it runs past and the animals it sees. One interesting way to do this is to actually reset the story in your own locality so that the mouse runs from the school kitchens, down to the corner shop, past the pub and so on. It is also fun to have children from the class in the story instead of the animals. You could do this by drawing a map of the local area and having the children's pictures on Velcro – so endless variations can be told!

Once upon a time there was a school cook who baked a gingerbread mouse. Unfortunately the gingerbread mouse ran out of the kitchen!

'Stop, stop little gingerbread man,' shouted the cook.

But the gingerbread mouse shouted, 'Run, run as fast as you can, you can't catch me I'm the gingerbread mouse.'

So the cook chased the gingerbread mouse down the school corridor till he came to class one.

'Stop, stop little gingerbread mouse,' shouted the teacher Mrs Jenkins.

The Enormous Turnip

Once upon a time there was a little old man who grew an enormous turnip.

Early one morning he decided to pull up the turnip to make turnip soup.

So, he pulled and he pulled and he pulled. But the turnip would not budge. Next he asked his wife to help.

So, the woman pulled the man and the man pulled the turnip. But still the turnip would not budge. Next he asked his son to help.

So, the son pulled the woman and the woman pulled the man and the man pulled the turnip. But still the turnip would not budge. Next he asked his daughter to help.

So, the daughter pulled the son and the son pulled the woman and the woman pulled the man and the little old man pulled the turnip. But still the turnip would not budge. Next he asked the dog to help.

So, the dog pulled the daughter and the daughter pulled the son and the son pulled the woman and the woman pulled the man and the little old man pulled the turnip. But still the turnip would not budge. Next he asked the cat to help.

So, the cat pulled the dog and the dog pulled the daughter and the daughter pulled the son and the son pulled the woman and the woman pulled the man and the little old man pulled the turnip. But still the turnip would not budge. Next he asked the mouse to help.

So, the mouse pulled the cat and the cat pulled the dog and the dog pulled the daughter and the daughter pulled the son and the son pulled the woman and the woman pulled the man and the little old man pulled the turnip. But still the turnip would not budge!

They pulled and they pulled and they pulled. Finally, the turnip came flying out of the ground and they all fell down with a BANG! After that they had turnip soup and lived happily ever after.

The Enormous Turnip Story Card

Once
time
was
little
old
who
grew
early
morning
decided
soup
so
pulled
would
budge
next
finally
happily
ever
after

The Enormous Turnip – ideas and innovations

Ideas
- What is a turnip?
- Different sorts of vegetables.
- Where do they grow?
- What are they used for?
- Printing with potatoes and other vegetables.
- Collage of vegetables.
- Farming in different parts of the world.
- Growing things – cress, beans.
- Plants need water and light.
- Size – bigger and bigger.
- Pulling and pushing.
- Hot seat characters.
- Draw everyone in a line pulling and show size difference.
- Tug of war!!! (If you dare) – perform in assembly!

Innovations

This is a great one to chant as different character all join onto each other and try pulling together. It would be easy enough to innovate upon – change the various people and creatures involved as well as the turnip – carrot, onion, leek would do. I suppose you could even struggle to pull something from a tree like an apple! Notice how in this innovation, I have not only substituted but began to add in a few extra descriptive words:

Once upon a time there was a little girl called Sandi who grew an enormous orange carrot.

Early one misty morning she decided to pull up the carrot to make carrot pie.

So, she pulled and she pulled and she pulled. But the carrot would not budge. Next she asked her big brother Carlos to help.

So, Carlos pulled Sandi and Sandi pulled the carrot. But still the turnip would not budge. Next she asked their old dog Billi to help.

Billy Goats Gruff

Once upon a time there was not one, not two but three 3 Billy Goats Gruff who lived beside a stream.

Early one morning they woke up and wanted to cross the bridge to eat some fresh green grass on the other side.

First baby Billy Goat Gruff went trip trap, trip trap over the bridge.
'Who goes trip trap, trip trap over my bridge?' said the Troll.
'It is I, Baby Billy Goat Gruff.'
'Then I'll eat you up,' replied the Troll gruffly.
'No, no – wait for my older brother. He is far fatter than I.'
So the Troll let Baby Billy Goat Gruff pass by.

Next middle-sized Billy Goat Gruff went trip trap, trip trap over the bridge.
'Who goes trip trap, trip trap over my bridge?' said the Troll.
'It is I, middle-sized Billy Goat Gruff.'
'Then I'll eat you up,' replied the Troll gruffly.
'No, no – wait for my older brother. He is far fatter than I.'
So the Troll let middle-sized Billy Goat Gruff pass by.

Finally Big Billy Goat Gruff went trip trap, trip trap over the bridge.
'Who goes trip trap, trip trap over my bridge?' said the Troll.
'It is I, Big Billy Goat Gruff.'
'Then I'll eat you up, ' replied the Troll gruffly.
'Oh no you won't!' said Big Billy Goat Gruff.
Big Billy Goat Gruff went trip trap, trip trap and BANGED the troll into the water with a mighty SPLASH!!

Finally, the three Billy Goats ate the fresh green grass and lived happily ever after.

The Billy Goats Gruff Story Card

Once
time
there
were
who
lived
beside
stream
woke
wanted
bridge
other
side
first
then
next
finally
older
brother
banged
happily
ever
after

The Billy Goats Gruff – ideas and innovations

Ideas
- What do animals eat?
- Dry rocky places and lush green places.
- Looking after sheep and goats, cows and horses.
- Farming and shepherds.
- Hills, valleys, streams.
- Bridges – who can build the sturdiest bridge?
- Fierce animals and 'baddies' – ogres, giants, dragons.
- Size – small, medium, and large.
- Changing voices – high, medium, deep.
- Troll or goat masks.
- Hot seat characters – interview troll!
- River animal's gossip about what has happened.

Innovations
This is a good story for children acting out the different parts and using different voices for each character. I once saw a finger puppet performance of this story – but the children had changed the goats into snowmen that wanted to cross the road to get into a freezer that was on the other side of the road! Make changes – and add in description.

Once upon a time there were not one, not two but three giant giraffes who lived beside a deep lake.

Early one sunny morning they woke up and wanted to cross the deep lake to eat some fresh leaves on a tall tree.

First baby giant giraffe went swishy swashy across the deep lake.

'Who goes swishy swashy across my lake?' said the Giant shark angrily.

'It is I, Baby giant giraffe.'

'Then I'll eat you up,' replied the Giant shark angrily.

'No, no – wait for my older brother. He is far fatter than I.'

Going For a Song

Once upon a time there was an old donkey who lived on the edge of a big city.

Unfortunately, his master said that he was too old to work any more so the donkey decided to leave home and go to sing in the city.

Next he walked and he walked and he walked till he came to a milking parlour. There he met a cow – who was too old to give milk!

'Where are you going?' asked the cow.

'I'm going to sing in the city,' said the donkey, 'so you can join me.'

'Let's sing,' said the donkey.

So the donkey brayed
and the cow mooed,

and everyone shouted, 'BE QUIET DOWN THERE, WE'RE TRYING TO SLEEP!'

So the donkey and the cow walked and they walked and they walked till they came to a cheese maker's shop. There they met a cat – who was too old to catch mice!

'Where are you going?' asked the cat.

'To sing in the city,' said the donkey, 'so you can join us.'

'Let's sing,' said the donkey.

So the donkey brayed
and the cow mooed,
and the cat meowed,

and everyone shouted, 'BE QUIET DOWN THERE, WE'RE TRYING TO SLEEP!'

So the donkey and the cow and the cat walked and they walked and they walked till they came to the baker's shop. There they met a dog – who was too old to guard the baker's shop.

'Where are you going?' asked the dog.

'To sing in the city,' said the donkey, 'so you can follow me.'

'Let's sing,' said the donkey.

So the donkey brayed
and the cow mooed,
and the cat meowed,
and the dog barked,

and everyone shouted, 'BE QUIET DOWN THERE, WE'RE TRYING TO SLEEP!'

So the donkey and the cow and the cat and the dog walked and they walked and they walked till they came to the city but unfortunately the city gate was shut.

'Let's sing,' said the donkey.

So the donkey brayed
and the cow mooed
and the cat meowed
and dog barked

and everyone in the city flung open their windows and shouted at the top of their voices, 'BE QUIET, WE'RE TRYING TO SLEEP!'

Finally, the donkey and the cow and the cat and the dog crept back home to rest their voices and their sleepy heads.

Going For a Song Story Card

Once
time
there
was
who
lived
unfortunately
owner
master
old
decided
leave
home
walked
came
there
next
where
so
quiet
we're
everyone
their
window
finally
voices
heads

Going for a song – ideas and innovations

Ideas
- Different creatures.
- Old/young animals and their names.
- Looking after old creatures/people.
- Hot seat characters.
- Gossip the next morning by people who were woken.
- Act out in hall all going on a journey.
- Sounds animals make – singing!

Innovations

A more challenging story to learn – see also the story of Kassim in the appendices. Make sure that they know it thoroughly before innovating. Then try changing characters, places, sounds they make – also add in extra description and maybe change the speech.

Once upon a time there was an old cat who lived near a tumbled down factory.

Unfortunately, her owner said that she was too old to work any more so the cat decided to leave home and go to sing in the city.

Next she walked and she walked and she walked till she came to a metal pylon. There she met a dog – who was too old to guard the house!

'Where are you going?' asked the dog noisily.

'I'm going to sing in the city,' said the cat, 'so you can join me.'

'Let's sing,' said the cat.

So the cat meowed
and the dog barked,

and everyone shouted, 'SHHHH WE ARE TRYING TO SLEEP UP HERE!'

Peter and the Wolf

Once upon a time there was a little boy called Peter who lived with his granddad on the edge of a big forest.

'Don't go out of the garden,' warned Peter's granddad, 'there is a wolf in the forest.'

But Peter went through the gate to play with his friends. Unfortunately, they were quarrelling by the pond.

First the bird said, 'You can't even fly!'

Next the duck said, 'You can't even swim!'

But at that moment along came ...

A cat – a lean cat, a mean cat.

The duck quacked angrily from the middle of the pond.
The bird squawked angrily from the top of the tree.

But at that moment along came ...

Grandad! – and he took Peter back into the house angrily!

But at that moment along came ...

A wolf!

First the cat spat and jumped up into a tree.
Next the bird shrieked and flew up into the tree.
Finally, the duck tried to swim away ...

But at that moment along came ...

Peter!
He lowered a rope from the top of the wall
and luckily he captured the wolf by his tail.

But at that moment along came ...

Not one, not two but three hunters,
bumbling and stumbling out of the forest.

'Don't shoot,' shouted Peter.
'I know where we should take him!'

Finally, Peter, the hunters, granddad, the bird and the cat all took the wolf to the zoo.

Luckily, the wolf was safe behind bars.

But late at night if you listen carefully, you might just hear the sound of the duck
quack, quack, quacking from inside his tummy!

Peter and the Wolf Story Card

Once
time
there
was
lived
with
warned
but
every
unfortunately
quarrelling
first
next
at that moment
along
came
angrily
captured
luckily
finally
safe
listen
carefully

Peter and the Wolf – ideas and innovations

Ideas

- Forests and wolves.
- Warnings about dangerous places and things.
- Disobeying.
- Friends – quarrelling.
- Ducks and birds.
- Zoos.
- Listening to the music and story on CD.
- Perform as a play.
- Hot seat characters – freeze frame and interview characters.
- Create dance for key moments.

Innovations

Learn this one thoroughly before moving on – it is worth it! Obviously you can make lots of changes – and keep adding in extra description where possible. Try inventing other warning stories about dangerous places or creatures. For innovation, you could totally reset the story:

Once upon a time there was a little girl called Simone who lived with her Mummy by the sea.

'Don't go onto the ragged rocks,' warned Simone's Mummy, 'there is a naughty mermaid.'

But every day Simone ran onto the ragged rocks to play with her friends. Unfortunately, they were quarrelling in a rock pool.

First the crab said, 'You can't even nip people's toes!'

Next the fish said, 'You can't even swim!'

Simone laughed at them for being so silly.

But at that moment along came ...

A cat – a tabby cat.

Monkey see – monkey do!

Once upon a time there was man who sold hats.

One day he was travelling through the forest when his cart hit a stone in the road.

Unfortunately, all the hats spilled out onto the road. As soon as the monkeys in the trees saw the hats, they swung down and grabbed them as quick as a click.

First the man shouted at the monkeys but all that the monkeys did was to shout back because – what a monkey sees, then a monkey does!

Next the man shook his fist at the monkeys but all that the monkeys did was to shake their fists back because – what a monkey sees, then a monkey does!

After that the man threw a stick at the monkeys but all that the monkeys did was to throw sticks back at the man because – what a monkey sees, then a monkey does!

Sadly, the man rubbed his eyes and began to cry but all that the monkeys did was to rub their eyes and cry because – what a monkey sees, then a monkey does!

Finally, the man was so fed up that he knew that he would never see his lovely hats again so he threw his own hat onto the ground and began to push his cart towards the city – but all that the monkeys did was to throw their hats onto the ground because – what a monkey sees, then a monkey does!

At that moment, the hat seller looked behind him and to his amazement all his hats were back on the ground.

He looked up into the trees but there was not a monkey to be seen.

They had all chased off to another part of the forest where one of them had seen a gingerbread man being chased – because whatever a monkey sees then a monkey does!

Four leaf clover –
My story is over!

Monkey See – Monkey Do! Story Card

Once
upon
time
there
was
sold
travelling
when
unfortunately
spilled
as soon as
first
next
after that
sadly
finally
at that moment
to his amazement

Monkey See – Monkey Do! – ideas and innovations

Ideas

- Copying actions – the mirror game where children are in pairs and have to copy each other's actions.
- Pictures of monkeys – monkey world
- Who was silliest?
- Story game – retell in a circle, a piece at a time, passing round a magic microphone.
- Perform the story with a hat seller, a narrator and lots of monkeys miming.
- Ideally use a large collection of hats.

Innovations

I seem to recall that this is a story from India – and it is one that I have known for ages. You will probably need to stick to monkeys for the innovation – though I suppose you could have parrots swooping down and stealing the hats – or some other sort of bird such as Cockatoos! Also – you will probably need to keep the hats – but the rest is open to changes of all sorts. If it is the first story of year 1, you may want to stick to substitutions with some additions.

Once upon a time there was a young traveller from Bombay who sold all sorts of clothes including – hats! Why he had hats of every type.

One sunny day he was travelling through the deep forest when his cart got stuck in a hole in the road.

Unfortunately, all the hats spilled out onto the dusty road. There were hats everywhere! As soon as the naughty monkeys in the trees saw the hats, they swung down and grabbed them as quick as a smack!

First the young traveller stamped his foot at the monkeys but all that the monkeys did was to stamp their feet back because – what a monkey sees, then a monkey does!

The Three Bears

Once upon a time there was a little girl called Goldilocks who lived in a village.

Early one morning she woke up and went for a walk in the forest.

Next she walked and she walked and she walked till she came to a little cottage. She knocked on the door and went in.

Inside she saw three bowls of steaming, sweet porridge.

'Mmmm, I'm hungry', said Goldilocks.

First she tasted the big bowl – but it was too hot.
Next she tasted the middle-sized bowl – but it was too cold.
Finally she tasted the baby-sized bowl – and that was just right.
So she ate all the porridge up!

After that she saw three chairs.
'I'm tired', said Goldilocks, stretching.

First she sat on the big chair – but it was too hard.
Next she sat on the middle-sized chair – but it was too soft.
Finally she sat on the baby-sized chair – and that was just right.
CRACK!
Suddenly the chair broke!

After that she saw three beds.
'Oh dear, I'm sleepy', said Goldilocks, yawning.

First she lay on the big bed – but it was too hard.
Next she lay on the middle-sized bed – but it was too soft.
Finally she lay on the baby-sized bed – and that was just right.
So, she fell fast asleep!

At that moment back came the three bears!

Firstly the big bear went to eat his porridge.
'Somebody's been eating my porridge.'

Next the middle-sized bear went to eat her porridge.
'Somebody's been eating my porridge.'

Finally the baby bear went to eat his porridge.
'Somebody's been eating my porridge and they've eaten it all up!'

After that the bears wanted to sit down!

First the big bear went to sit on his big chair.
'Somebody's been sitting in my chair.'

Next the middle-sized bear went to sit on her middle-sized chair.
'Somebody's been sitting in my chair.'

Finally the baby bear went to sit on his chair.
'Somebody's been sitting on my chair – and they've broken it!

After that the bears felt sleepy.

First the big bear went to sleep in his big bed.
'Somebody's been sleeping in my bed.'

Next the middle-sized bear went to sleep in her middle-sized bed.
'Somebody's been sleeping in my bed.'

Finally the baby bear went to sleep in his baby bed.
'Somebody's been sleeping in my bed – and she's still there!

Goldilocks woke up and SCREAMED!

So she ran and she ran and she ran as fast as a cheetah until in the end she ran all the way home. The three bears lived happily ever after.

The Three Bears Story Card

Once upon a time
there
was
who
early one morning
walk
next
knocked
inside
saw
first
finally
middle-sized
baby-sized
tasted
right
so
after that
tired
suddenly
fast asleep
at that moment
somebody
screamed
happily ever after

The Three Bears – ideas and innovations

Ideas

■ Sing 'When Goldilocks came to the House of 3 Bears'

■ Read – or tell 'We're going on a bear hunt' which is not really by Michael Rosen – he has rewritten what is actually an old story!

■ Point out how in stories things often happen in of 3's. This makes a good structure for storymaking.

■ Create a 3 bears cave in the classroom.

■ Explore comparisons – size, heat and touch.

■ Hot seat bears and Goldilocks – what excuses does she have?

■ What did her mummy say when she got home – write a letter of apology to the bears.

■ Freeze frame at key moments;

■ Bear masks for acting story out.

Innovations

Make sure that innovations include substitutions but also add in extra description or dialogue. Try making more of the opening – think about how Goldilocks would have felt for instance. If not bears – what other creatures? Where are they living – try modernising the story. (It is basically a 'break and entry' story – so you could make up other stories in which someone goes somewhere forbidden.)

Once upon a time there was a little boy called Billi. One day his Mum sent him down to the shops to buy some bread. He walked and he walked and he walked till he came to the shop. There was no-one there so he went in to wait for the bakers.
Inside he saw 3 large loaves of bread. 'Mmmm, I'm hungry', said Billi …

Try retelling from a bear's view: *Mum had made the porridge so hot that it needed to cool down so we went out for a walk. When we got back …*

Or Goldi telling her Mum: *I was lost in the forest so I went into this little cottage. It was so dark that at first I couldn't see anything but then I noticed some bowls on the table. I felt so hungry that I was tempted to …*

The Three Little Pigs

This is the story of the three little pigs and this is the way that we tell it.

Once upon a time there were three little pigs who lived with their mother.

Early one morning they woke up and their mother said, 'You're too big for this house and it's time you left home.'

So they walked and they walked and they walked.

The first pig made a house out of straw.

Unfortunately, a wolf came creeping by.

'Little pig, little pig, let me come in.'
'No, no, no by the hairs on my chinny chin chin, I'll not let you in.'
'Then I'll huff and I'll puff and I'll blow your house in.'
So the wolf huffed and he puffed and he blew the house in.

So the first little pig ran away to find his brothers.

Now the second little pig had made his house out of sticks.

Unfortunately, the wolf came creeping by.

'Little pig, little pig, let me come in.'
'No, no, no by the hairs on my chinny chin chin, I'll not let you in.'
'Then I'll huff and I'll puff and I'll blow your house in.'
So the wolf huffed and he puffed and he blew the house in.

So the first little pig and the second little pig ran away to find their brother.

Now the third little pig had made his house out of bricks.

Unfortunately, the wolf came creeping by.

'Little pig, little pig, let me come in.'
'No, no, no by the hairs on my chinny chin chin, I'll not let you in.'
'Then I'll huff and I'll puff and I'll blow your house in.'
So he huffed and he puffed and he huffed and he puffed and he huffed and he puffed but luckily he could not blow the house in.

The wolf was so angry that he climbed onto the roof and began to climb down the chimney.

The third little pig hung a pot full of boiling water over a blazing fire. Just as the wolf was coming down the chimney they took off the cover!

In fell the wolf.

He shot back out of that chimney and he ran and he ran and he ran all the way home with his tail between his legs and his bottom as red as a radish.

Now from that day to this those three little pigs have lived happily ever after.

The Three Little Pigs

Once upon a time
there
were
three
little
who
lived
with
their
early one morning
woke
said
house/home
walked
first
second
third
unfortunately/luckily
huffed/puffed
blew
brother
angry
climb
chimney
now
happily ever after

The Three Little Pigs – ideas and innovations

Ideas

■ This is another of the most common and well-known tales so everyone should know it.
■ Farm animals.
■ Houses and buildings.
■ Building materials – making mini houses with straw, sticks, leggo.
■ Try using a hair dryer as the wolf to test which buildings stand best.
■ Make mini houses out of shoeboxes.
■ Hot seat the wolf and ask him about his bad behaviour.
■ Interview the three pigs about what happened to them.
■ List 5 ways to trap a wolf!
■ Letter of apology from wolf – pigs phone their mum!
■ Find out about real wolves.

Innovations

Try starting with a simple substitution plus some addition.

Once upon a time there were three tabby cats who lived with their mother. One afternoon they set off to seek their fortune. They walked and they walked and they walked.
Now the first tabby cat made a house out of lollipop sticks.
Unfortunately, a grumpy dog came growling by. 'Little cat, little cat, let me come in.'
'No, no, no by the hairs on my chinny chin chin, I'll not let you in.'
'Then I'll huff and I'll puff and I'll blow your house in.' So the grumpy dog huffed and he puffed and he blew the house in.

Then move onto trying out things like what would happen if it was a nice wolf and he made friends with the cats and they all visited each other? Suppose the four friends then met a nasty snake?

Now the first little cat tried to make a house out of straw. Luckily a friendly wolf came by and helped the tabby cat. The two friends had tea but at that moment they heard a spiteful snake slithering closer and closer and closer.

The Magic Porridge Pot

Once not twice but once upon a time there was a little girl called Poppy who lived with her poor old mother.

Early one morning she was walking in the woods when she helped an old lady carry her bags home. So the kind old lady gave her a magic porridge pot.

'Say the words, 'Cook, little pot, cook' and it will give you hot porridge. But once you have eaten enough, say 'Stop, little pot, stop', or it will carry on cooking.'

Poppy ran home and showed her mother.

'Cook, little pot, cook' said Poppy
Soon the pot was full of hot, sweet porridge.
'Stop, little pot, stop,' said Poppy,
and the porridge stopped cooking.

One day Poppy was visiting her grandma when her mother felt hungry.

'Cook, little pot, cook,' said her mother.
Soon the pot was full of sweet porridge as hot as boiling soup.
Unfortunately, she could not remember the words to make the pot stop!

Oh dear there was porridge, porridge everywhere –
The porridge poured –
out of the pot,
onto the floor,
up the stairs
and out of the door
into the rooms
and down the lane
until there was porridge, porridge everywhere.

When Poppy came back she shouted out,
'Stop, little pot, stop!'

Luckily, the pot stopped.

In then end everyone had to eat porridge for a whole month and they lived happily ever after!

The Magic Porridge Pot

Once upon a time
there was little girl/boy called
who lived with
early one morning
walking
where
gave
magic
porridge
but
have
eaten enough
showed
when
felt hungry
soon
as
unfortunately
remember
words
poured
everywhere
when
shouted
luckily
everyone lived happily ever after

The Magic Porridge Pot – ideas and innovations

Ideas

- It's surprising how many stories involve animals, growing things or cooking! I've known this story ever since I was tiny and I am still haunted by the idea of something that gets out of control – it reminds me of the story of the Lambton Worm – which if cut in half, just grows two larger halves, ever increasing in size.
- Cooking and recipes.
- Creating imaginary recipes.
- Sweetening things – healthy eating.
- Why did the lady give her the pot?
- Try singing the refrain 'out of the pot/onto the floor.
- Interview Poppy and Mum and a villager who saw the events.
- Write the story as a news item or report it on TV!

Innovations

This is a lovely story to innovate – change the people, the setting, the container and instead of porridge, why not have – soup or stew? You could add in why the old lady helped Poppy with the pot – in most versions of this tale the child performs some deed of kindness and the pot is a reward (see the Magic Brush in year 2 which uses the same idea).

Once upon a time when the world was fine – there was a little girl called Rifat who lived with her poor old granny.

Late one wintry afternoon she was walking to the shops when she saw a poor old lady hobbling along. So Rifat helped her all the way home. In return for her kindness the old lady gave Rifat a magic soup saucepan.

'Say the words, 'Cook, saucy saucepan, cook' and it will give you steaming hot soup. But once you have eaten enough, you must say 'Stop, little saucepan, stop.'

Rifat ran home and showed her granny.

'Cook, saucy saucepan, cook' said Rifat ...

How tortoise got his shell

Once upon a time the birds did not know how to fly. But one day crow discovered that if he flapped his wings, he soared high above the trees.

First he told tiger but tiger just roared!
Next he told elephant but elephant just blew his trumpet!
After that he told giraffe but giraffe just laughed!
Finally he told his friend tortoise who believed him.

So the two friends decided to climb to the top of the mountain to show all the birds how to fly.

So they climbed and they climbed and they climbed till they came to the top of the mountain.

First crow jumped off the top and spread his wings so that he soared high above the clouds.

All the birds cheered noisily!

Then silly old tortoise decided to help his friend so he too jumped off the top.

At that moment, he realised that he did not have any wings. He tumbled down and down and down ... until he smashed on the rocks below.

Immediately, all the birds of the air flew down to help tortoise.

And so it is to this very day that you can still see where all the birds of the air put tortoise's shell back together again, piece by piece.

How Tortoise Got His Shell

Once upon a time
birds
how
discovered
soared
high
first
next
after
that
finally
laughed/believed
decided
climb
then
friend
at that moment
realised
tumbled
below
immediately
where
very
together
again
piece

How Tortoise Got His Shell – ideas and innovations

Ideas
- Crows and tortoises – unlikely friends!
- Show images of a crow and a tortoise
- Especially so children can see crisscross pattern on shell.
- Myths – explain 'how' or 'why'.
- Wings – flight.
- Tortoise collage to show crisscross pattern on back.
- Have two other animals gossiping about how silly crow has been pretending he can fly.
- Have two animals talking about what they saw tortoise do!
- Friendship theme.

Innovations

A simple substitution – though I suspect that you will have to keep the tortoise because of the shell pattern. You could add in plenty of extra description, e.g.

Once upon a time the birds did not know how to fly. But one day crow was standing on a rock. It was so hot that he began to flap his wings. The more he flapped, the cooler he grew. Suddenly he flapped so quickly that to his amazement he began to fly! He soared high above the trees …

You could think of other animals that have distinguishing marks and invent stories about 'how' they came about these features, e.g. 'How camel got his hump', 'How cat began to purr', or 'How Tiger got his stripes'.

Once upon a time the tigers did not have stripes. They were yellow all over.

One day tiger was out in the forest when he heard someone setting up a barbecue! Mmmm, that smelled so good that he decided to go and see what was cooking …

Rumplestiltskin

Now once upon a time in the land where icicles grow all summer there lived a silly miller who boasted to the King that his daughter Rosalind could spin straw into gold.

So the King put Rosalind into a room at the top of a tall tower and told her to spin one bale of straw into gold by morning or she would never see the light of day again.

Sadly, Rosalind cried and cried because she knew that she could not spin straw into gold.

As soon as she started to cry a little old man appeared who said, 'Wipe away your tears, put away your fears, if you give me your necklace, I will spin the straw into gold.'

By next morning the straw was gold.

But the King just gave her not one but two bales of straw to spin into gold.

Sadly, Rosalind cried and cried because she knew that she could not spin straw into gold.

As soon as she started to cry a little old man appeared who said, 'Wipe away your tears, put away your fears, if you give me your ring, I will spin the straw into gold.'

By next morning the straw was gold.

But the King just gave her not one not two but three bales of straw to spin into gold.

Sadly, Rosalind cried and cried because she knew that she could not spin straw into gold.

As soon as she started to cry a little old man appeared who said, 'Wipe away your tears, put away your fears if you give me your first baby I will spin the straw into gold.'

By next morning the straw was gold.

Luckily, the King was so pleased with all the gold that he married Rosalind.

After a year a baby boy was born.

That night the little old man appeared to take away the baby.

Rosalind cried and cried because she did not want to lose the baby.

'To keep the child, you must guess my name,' said the little old man.

One night later, he appeared – but Rosalind could not guess his name.

Two nights later, he appeared – but Rosalind could not guess his name.

On the third day a woodcutter overheard the little old man singing,
'Rosalind will loose this game,
 for Rumplestiltskin is my name!'

and he told Rosalind.

That night the little old man appeared.

'Is your name Zambola?'
'Never!' screamed the little old man.
'Is you name Gambobambo?'
'Never!' screamed the little old man.
'Then it must be – Rumplestiltskin!'

Angrily, the little old man stamped and he stamped and he stamped his foot so hard that he shot through the floor right into the middle of the earth and was never seen again!

But Rosalind and the King and the baby lived happily ever after.

Rumplestiltskin Story Card

Once upon a time
there lived
who
daughter
could
straw/bale
so
morning
sadly
cried
knew
as soon as
appeared
said
tears/fears
by next morning
first
baby
luckily
pleased
after a year
born
guess
name
night
later
overheard
lived happily ever after

Rumplestiltskin – ideas and innovations

Ideas
- Boasting – and greed!
- Who was the worst character?
- Discuss puzzles and patterns, likes and dislikes.
- Hot seat the characters.
- Hot seat the boastful miller about what he has done to his daughter.
- Try retelling the tale from the King's viewpoint.
- Dress up in a crown and cloak.
- Freeze frame at key moment and interview characters.
- Draw characters and place on wall.
- Add to drawings what we know about different characters.
- Invent ideas about Rumplestiltskin's life.
- Spinning and weaving.
- Make Rosalind's necklace or ring.

Innovations
Begin with a simple substitution and then add in some description ...

Sadly, Rosalind cried and cried because she knew that she could not spin straw into gold. The room was dark and shadows from the candle light flickered.

As soon as she started to cry a little old man appeared. He seemed to come out of nowhere. He stared at her with beady eyes and said, 'Wipe away your tears, put away your fears, if you give me your necklace, I will spin the straw into gold.'

The Papaya that spoke

Once upon a time there was farmer who lived in a village. One day he felt hungry so he went out to pick a papaya. To his amazement, the papaya spoke, 'Hands off!'

The farmer looked at his dog. 'Did you say that?' said the farmer.
'No,' said the dog, 'it was the papaya!'
'Aaaaargh!' screamed the farmer. As fast as his legs could carry him, he ran and he ran and he ran till he came to a market where he met a fisherman selling fish.

'Why are you running so fast when the sun is shining so bright?' asked the fisherman.
'First a papaya spoke to me and next my dog!' replied the farmer.
'That's impossible,' said the fisherman.
'Oh no it isn't,' said one of the fish.

'Aaaaargh!' screamed the farmer. As fast as his legs could carry him, he ran and he ran and he ran till he came to a field where he met a shepherd with his goats.

'Why are you running so fast when the sun is shining so bright?' asked the shepherd.
'First a papaya spoke to me, next my dog and after that a fish!' replied the farmer.
'That's impossible,' said the fisherman.
'Oh no it isn't,' bleated one of the goats.

'Aaaaargh!' screamed the farmer. As fast as his legs could carry him, he ran and he ran and he ran till he came to the village where he met the King sitting on his old wooden rocking chair.

'Why are you running so fast when the sun is shining so bright?' asked the King.
'First a papaya spoke to me, next my dog, after that a fish and finally a goat!'
'That's impossible,' said the King. 'Get out of here you foolish man.' So the poor farmer walked home with his head hung down. The King rocked back and forth, back and forth, back and forth. 'How silly of him to imagine that things could talk.' There was a long silence – and then suddenly – the chair spoke! 'Quite so – whoever heard of a talking papaya?'

The Papaya That Spoke Story Card

Once upon a time
there was
who lived
hungry
to his amazement
spoke
fast
why
first
next
after that
finally
replied
impossible
imagine
things
speak
there was
silence
suddenly

The Papaya that Spoke – ideas and innovations

Ideas

- What is a papaya – very nice with a squeeze of lime!
- Where do they grow and how?
- Cut in half and draw fruit – pencil and pastel.
- Slice fruit up and use for printing.
- Make a fruit salad – healthy eating.
- Recipe for fruit salads.
- Survey to discover favourite fruits – bar chart.
- Hot seat characters.
- Hold advice session – what should the farmer do?
- Act story out and perform for assembly.

Innovations

For young children this is just a funny story – but it is also a sort of ghost story in which a person hears things speak or sees objects move. No one listens – but in the end there is the twist when the person 'in charge' experiences the same thing. Try a simple substitution and addition, at first only making a few changes.

Once upon a time there was farmer who lived near a well. One day he felt hungry so he went out to pick an apple. To his amazement, the apple spoke, 'Hands off!'

Then tell it again but reset it completely and add in more description, e.g.

Once upon a time there was a boy called Clarence who lived in Manchester. One day his dad told Clarence to take the dog for a walk and to go and buy a newspaper. To Clarence's amazement as soon as he touched the paper, it spoke, 'Put me down!'

Clarence stared at the paper as if it was on fire and then he began to run down the street screaming his head off. He ran and he ran and he ran all the way down to the corner shop where ...

How the world was made

Once upon a time there was no sun, no moon, no stars. There was only darkness.

On the first day of the week the piper began to bang his great bass drum like thunder beating and the mountains appeared, one by one.

On the second day of the week the piper began to play his flute like songbirds singing and the rivers flowed down the hills and into the sea.

On the third day of the week the piper began to bang his silver cymbals like storm waves clashing and the forests appeared, flowing like water over the land.

On the fourth day of the week the piper began to play his violin like the wind singing in the trees and the grasses grew and swept like waves across the earth.

On the fifth day of the week the piper began to strum his guitar like the rhythm of the rain and with each note a new creature appeared.

On the sixth day of the week the piper began to click his castanets like bony fingers snapping and man and woman grew in the forest.

On the last day of the week the piper began to sing like a thousand choirs and as the piper sang the sun, the moon and finally the stars appeared one by one in the great open skies.

So the world began.

How the World was Made Story Card

How
world
earth
planets
sky
universe
made
once upon a time
there was
only
darkness
first second third fourth fifth sixth seventh
week
mountains rivers oceans forests trees
animals/creatures
man
woman
grasses
rocks
plants
flowers
rain/snow/storms/thunder/lightning
sun/moon/stars/earth/planets
world
began

How the World was Made – ideas and innovations

Ideas
- Creation myths – discuss any other creation stories the children know.
- Notice use of similes – try inventing new similes, e.g. the moon is like ... ... , the sun is like ... ...
- List and add more geographical features.
- Different places in the world have different features – flora and fauna.
- Musical instruments from around the world.
- Play game guessing in which a sound is made by different instruments – on a tape or play behind a curtain.
- Make homemade shakers and bangers.
- What sound might bring into being what animal, plant or feature?
- Set a rhythmic beat or simple 3 chime bar melody as a background to the story.
- Tell the story chorally – with different groups saying different days of the week – perform for assembly – using instruments.
- Days of the week.

Innovations
The simple pattern of this lends itself to making a simple and well-illustrated book for each child.

Once upon a time there was no earth, no sky, no creatures. There was only darkness.

On the first day of the week the music maker began to play her piccolo like silver bells chiming and the birds appeared, one by one.

On the second day of the week the music maker began to play her harp like the waves on the shore and the earth began to blossom.

Cat, Bramble and Heron

Once upon a time there were three friends – Cat, Bramble and Heron who lived by a lake.

Early one morning they went out to seek their fortune.

First Bramble slithered through the grass but all that he found was a rusty old pot. Next Cat sneaked along by the wall but all that he found was an old fishbone. Finally, Heron flew down the road where he spied a pile of gold.

So Heron, Cat and Bramble divided the gold into not one, not two but three bags. Then they decided to hide their gold.

First, Heron spread out his wings, took the bag in his beak and flew high over the lake. Unfortunately, he saw his reflection in the water below. He thought that it was his brother so he called out, 'Hello,' and as soon as he opened his beak, the gold scattered down like rain.

Next, Cat crept along the wall and paused by a small hole. Unfortunately, Mr Mouse sneaked out and stole Cat's gold.

Finally, Bramble slithered along the hedgerows. Unfortunately, a thief sneaked by and stole Bramble's bag of gold.

And that is why to this very day, Cat is still waiting outside Mr Mouse's hole.

And that is why to this very day; Bramble snatches and grabs at your legs as you pass by.

And that is why to this very day, Heron is standing still in the water forever staring, still looking, looking, looking for his lost bag of gold.

Cat, Bramble and Heron Story Card

Once upon a time
there were
three friends
who lived
early one morning
seek their fortune
first
next
finally
but all that he/she found
was
where
divided
one/two/three
then
decided
hide
their
unfortunately
reflection
thought
brother
like
called
thief/stole
that
why

Cat, Bramble and Heron – ideas and innovations

Ideas

- What is a bramble – what do they look like – essential before starting the story!
- Also – what is a heron and how do they feed?
- Look at language used – identify powerful words;
- Identify similes – and make up some more;
- Discuss 'luck' – who was lucky or unlucky in the story?
- How did it all go wrong?
- Hot seat characters – Discuss ending.

Innovations

I first heard this from a storyteller and I think that it originally comes from Wales. I cannot actually recall the original so this is my innovation based vaguely on what I remember! To innovate and change the three characters some careful thought will be needed. Each character will have to have some way of connecting to the end, e.g. thorns could snag at clothes; a dog might pause to check out a bone; a badger might stop to dig up a worm; a cuckoo might stop to rob a nest ...

Anyway – here is the beginning retold keeping to the original but with all the effort going into the addition of more description:

Once upon a time there were three friends – Cat, Bramble and Heron who lived by a lake. In the summer they lounged at the edge of the lake and Heron brought Cat plenty of fish to eat. In the winter Bramble built a shelter and kept Cat from the snow. In the spring Cat guarded Heron's nest from the fox and the stoat. So as you can see, they all were the best of friends.

Now early one morning they went out to seek their fortune.

First Bramble slithered through the tall grass by the lake's edge but all that he found was a rusty old pot. Then he crept up the pathway to the old boathouse but all that he found was a few old crisp packets ...

Greedy Fox

Early one morning Mr Fox woke up. He picked up his bag and went out to visit his lady friend.

He walked and walked and he walked till he came to the town pond. There he saw a frog. 'Mmmm,' he thought, 'that would make a nice present.' So, he grabbed the frog and popped it into his bag.

He walked and he walked and walked and he walked till he came to the candlestick makers. He knocked on the door and went straight in.

He said to the candlestick maker, 'May I leave my bag here while I visit my Uncle?'

'Of course you can,' said the candlestick maker.

'Very well,' said Mr Fox, 'but there is one thing while I am gone, *mind you don't look in my bag*.' Then he walked down the path, turned the corner and disappeared out of sight.

However, the candlestick maker grew curious. He opened the bag and out hopped the frog! A large brown rat pounced onto the frog and ate it up in one huge gulp.

Unfortunately, at that moment back came Mr Fox. 'Where is my frog?'

'I'm sorry,' said the candlestick maker, 'I opened up your bag and it hopped out and that large brown rat ate it up!'

'Right,' said the Fox. 'I'll have the rat instead.' So he grabbed the rat, shoved it into the bag and off he went.

He walked and he walked and he walked till he came to the bakers. He knocked on the door and went straight in.

He said to the baker, 'May I leave my bag here while I visit my Uncle? There is one thing while I am gone, *mind you don't look in my bag*.' Then he walked down the path, turned the corner and disappeared out of sight.

However, the baker grew curious. He opened the bag and out shot the rat! It shot out into the backyard and was chased off by the baker's puppy!

Unfortunately, at that moment back came Mr Fox. 'Where is my rat?'

'I'm sorry,' said the baker, 'I opened up your bag and it ran out into the backyard. My puppy's chased it off!'

'Right,' said the Fox. 'I'll have your puppy instead.' So he grabbed the puppy, shoved it into the bag and off he went.

He walked and he walked and he walked till he came to the butchers. He knocked on the door and went straight in.

He said to the butcher, 'May I leave my bag here while I visit my Uncle? There is one thing while I am gone, *mind you don't look in my bag.*' Then he walked down the path, turned the corner and disappeared out of sight.

However, the butcher grew curious. He opened the bag and out shot the puppy! It ran into the farmyard and was chased off by a little boy – whack, whack!

Unfortunately, at that moment back came Mr Fox. 'Where is my puppy?'

'I'm sorry,' said the little butcher, 'I opened the bag and it ran out into the farmyard and my boy chased it off!'

'Right,' said the fox. 'I'll have ...... some meat instead.' So he grabbed a leg of lamb that was on the table, shoved it into the bag and off he went.

He walked and he walked and he walked. Before long, one by one the dogs of the town began to follow him. They could smell the fresh meat in the bag. Soon he had twenty dogs following him, then thirty dogs, then forty. They began barking at his heels so he ran and he ran and he ran,
Out of the town, out of the town,
Over the down, over the down,
Across the lea, across the lea,
Down to the sea, down to the sea

And as far as I know Mr Fox is still running to this day,
still chased by that pack of dogs.

Mr Fox and his Bag Story Card

Early one morning
woke
walked
till/until
there
thought
knocked
straight
path
corner
disappeared
out of sight
however
grew curious
unfortunately
at that moment
grabbed/running
shoved/chased
still

The Fox and his Bag – ideas and innovations

Ideas

- Other sack stories?
- Discuss likes, dislikes, puzzles and patterns.
- Hot seat characters.
- Role-play Mr Fox's visit to his uncle's house.
- List what could go in the bag and where Mr Fox might travel.
- Discuss ending.
- Draw wall map of the journey.
- Act story out in small groups.
- Foxes – urban and country – how do they live?
- What do foxes eat – fact file on foxes.
- Other nighttime creatures – fox, badger, owl and bat.
- Read other foxy stories.

Innovations

This is probably a story from America. I have known it for years and it always makes a good one to tell. There is something ominous about that bag and of course towards the end the children think that Mr Fox is going to put the boy into the bag. Try retelling it as a substitution – maybe a wolf, tiger, coyote, bear, eagle – and put different creatures into the bag. Then focus on the ending and see what alternative ideas there might be, e.g.

'Right,' said the fox. 'I'll have some meat instead. So he grabbed a leg of lamb, shoved it into the bag and off he went.

He walked and he walked and he walked till he came to a water trough in the middle of the town. Mr Fox was thirsty so he put his bag down and had a long, cool drink. As soon as his back was turned the butcher, the baker and the candlestick maker took out the meat and popped in some stones. Then they went home to have roast meat for supper while Mr Fox had hard old stones that broke his teeth and made his tummy ache!

The Magic Brush

Long, long ago in China there lived a poor boy called Chang.
Although he loved drawing, Chang was too poor to have a paintbrush so he used a stick. He would draw in the sand or scratch marks on walls.

Early one morning Chang saw a large, silver fish trapped in the reeds by the riverbank. The fish was struggling to get free. Because Chang felt sorry for the fish, he helped to release it.

Later that day Chang was sleeping. In his dream a man dressed in a silver cloak spoke to him. 'You are a kind boy Chang. I am giving you a magic brush. Use it to help the poor.' Chang woke with a start and lying beside him was a paintbrush.

So Chang painted the shape of a butterfly and it changed into a real butterfly and flew away. Chang was amazed with his gift and ran straight back to the village to see how he could help the poor people.

First, he painted a donkey for the young mother to help her carry her goods. Next he painted an ox to help the farmer pull his plough. After that he painted a hoe for the old lady to weed her garden. Everyday he found a new use for the paintbrush.

Unluckily, the emperor heard of Chang and his magic brush. He sent for Chang and ordered him to paint a field of gold. Chang didn't want to obey the greedy emperor so he drew a sea with a tiny island in the distance.

'Where is my field of gold?' shouted the emperor, angrily.

'Just here,' replied Chang drawing a tiny field on the island.

'Paint me a boat so that I can travel to the island,' snarled the emperor. So Chang painted a boat. The emperor climbed onto the boat. Chang drew the north wind blowing towards the island.

'I'm going too slowly,' roared the emperor. 'Paint stronger wind.'

So Chang drew a storm. Suddenly, the waves grew rougher until the boat capsized and the emperor disappeared. The Chang drew a white horse so that he could ride home and tell his friends what had happened to the emperor who wanted too much for himself.

The Magic Brush Story Card

Long ago there lived
called
although
draw/drew/paint
early one morning
when
saw
trapped/struggling
free/rescue/release
because
helped
later that day
dream
magic
help the poor
lying beside
changed
real
amazed
first/next/after that/everyday
unluckily
ordered
island
distance
where/there/here
angrily/slowly/quickly/greedily/suddenly
what had happened
who

The Magic Brush – ideas and innovations

Ideas

- This is a Chinese story – where is China – what do we know about it? Dress up as the emperor. Use paintbrush as a prop.
- What other stories are there in which someone is kind and gets a reward (3 wishes, the magic porridge pot). Read these and discuss similarities.
- What other 'good deeds' could Chang do with his brush?
- What good deeds do we do?
- If we had Chang's brush what would we do?
- Helping others – charity.
- Gossip – people in the village talking about what has happened.
- Role-play the emperor receiving news about Chang.
- 'Thoughts in the head' – what in the emperor thinking?
- Hot seat the characters – freeze frame key scenes.
- Write in role – letter, diary or news report.
- Does the emperor deserve his ending?
- Paint some of the scenes that Chang paints for display.
- Learn and perform the story.

Innovations

I love this story – it has all the elements of a good tale – helping the poor, kindness, magic and a real baddie who needs to be put firmly in his place. Start with a simple substitution and add in description. Try then moving on to changing the setting so that the story has a different location. What might happen if Chang used the brush for mischievous acts – playing tricks on people? What other creature might Chang rescue? In my version, he saves a fish – there is another story that I tell in key stage 2 in which a poor fisherman also rescues a fish and is granted one wish.

Long, long ago in Wales there lived a poor boy called David.
Although he loved drawing, David was too poor to have a paintbrush so he used a stick. He would draw in the earth or scratch marks on walls.

Early one morning when David was walking to school, he saw a golden eagle trapped in the brambles. The golden eagle was struggling to get free. Because David felt sorry for the eagle, he helped to release it.

The Hobyahs

Once upon a time there was a little old man and a little old woman and their dog Turpy.

Late one night the hobyahs came, creeping through the long grass, calling, calling.

'Hobyah, hobyah – tear down the hemp stalks, carry off the little old woman.'

Luckily, the little dog Turpy, he barked so loudly that he frightened the hobyahs away. But the little old man said, 'If little dog Turpy doesn't stop that barking, I'll cut off his tail!'

The next night the hobyahs came back, creeping through the long grass, calling, calling.

'Hobyah, hobyah – tear down the hemp stalks, carry off the little old woman.'

Luckily, the little dog Turpy, he barked so loudly that he frightened the hobyahs away. But the little old man cut off little dog Turpy's tail and said, 'If little dog Turpy doesn't stop that barking, I'll cut off his legs!'

The next night the hobyahs came back, creeping through the long grass, calling, calling.

'Hobyah, hobyah – tear down the hemp stalks, carry off the little old woman.'

Luckily, the little dog Turpy, he barked so loudly that he frightened the hobyahs away. But the little old man cut off little dog Turpy's legs and said, 'If little dog Turpy doesn't stop that barking, I'll cut off his tongue!'

The next night the hobyahs came back, creeping through the long grass, calling, calling.

'Hobyah, hobyah – tear down the hemp stalks, carry off the little old woman.'

Luckily, the little dog Turpy, he barked so loudly that he frightened the hobyahs away. But the little old man cut off little dog Turpy's tongue and said, 'If little dog Turpy doesn't stop that barking, I'll cut off his head!'

The next night the hobyahs came back, creeping through the long grass, calling, calling.

'Hobyah, hobyah – tear down the hemp stalks, carry off the little old woman.'

Luckily, the little dog Turpy, he barked so loudly that he frightened the hobyahs away. But the little old man cut off poor little dog Turpy's head and said, 'At long last we can get some sleep!'

The next night the hobyahs came back, creeping through the long grass, calling calling.

'Hobyah, hobyah – tear down the hemp stalks, carry off the little old woman.'

They tore down the hempstalks and carried off the little old woman.

The next day the little old man put little dog Turpy back together again and they both waited.

That night the hobyahs came back, creeping through the long grass, calling, calling.

'Hobyah, hobyah – tear down the hemp stalks, carry off the little old man.'

So little dog Turpy, he barked so loudly that he frightened the hobyahs away. Next he ran and he ran and he ran till he found their cave. Luckily, he saved the little old woman and they went home.

The little old man said, 'Little dog Turpy can bark as long as he likes.' And so they all lived happily ever after.

The Hobyahs Story Card

Once upon a time
there was
little old woman/man
their
late one night
Hobyahs
came calling
tear down the hemp stalks
barking so loudly
that frightened
away/off
tail/legs/ears/tongue/head
but/next/at long last/the next night
tore down
carry/carried off
back together again
waited
luckily
saved
home
happily ever after

The Hobyahs – ideas and innovations

Ideas
- Hot seating and freeze frame.
- Discuss dislikes, likes, puzzles and patterns.
- Paint Hobyahs.
- Make Wanted Posters for Hobyahs.
- Hobyah masks for retelling.
- Create a dance for Hobyahs.
- Set to simple percussion or music using chime bars.
- Find out what hemp is and what it is used for.
- What other stories do we know that features a sack or bag?
- Hot seat old man at the end to find out how he feels about Turpy and how his feelings have changed.

Innovations

When I first used this story many teachers put it to one side and didn't bother with it. The general view was that it was one step too far. However, I had remembered my father telling me the story some 45 years before and I was sure that if it had been that memorable for me then it had to have something about it. A while later Sarah, a reception teacher, told me that her class had loved it – and on a visit to a farm they had all been on a trailer being drawn by a tractor when they went past a field of green wheat waving in the wind. 'Look Miss – hemp stalks!' called out one excited lad – and the next thing she knew, the whole class were chanting the story as they stared at what they thought were hemp stalks ...

I think most children have seen cartoons in which characters are flattened, stretched, dissected and have holes drilled through them – so the idea of taking a dog apart and putting it back together is actually rather tame stuff. The Hobyahs are actually the bit that is potentially scarier! When innovating you will still need a guard dog I think – but otherwise concentrate on substitutions, addition of more description and maybe changing the ending

Appendices

Reception Story Making Language Bank

Introduce
Once upon a time
Early one morning
And
Then
Next
Until/till
But
So
Finally

... who ...

'Run' (he walked and he walked ...)

Description – a lean cat, a mean cat ...

Alliteration

Adverbs: Luckily/unfortunately

Prepositions: down, into, over, out, onto.

Appendices

Year 1 Story Making Language Bank

Consolidate

Once upon a time
Early one morning
And
Then
Next
Until/till
But
So
Finally
... who ...

Introduce

After/after that
At that moment
Because
By the next morning
In the end
If......
First
Now

One day
Soon/ as soon as
Suddenly
To his amazement

... that ...
... or ...
... so that ...
... when ...
... where ...
... happily ever after

'Run' (he walked and he walked ...)
Description – a lean cat ...
Alliteration
Adverbs: Luckily/unfortunately
Prepositions: down, into, over, out, onto

Repetition for effect
Adjectives to describe
Simile – using 'as'
Adverbs: Suddenly, immediately
Prepositions: Inside, towards

Year 2 Story Making Language Bank

Consolidate

Once upon a time
Early one morning
One day
And
First
Next
Then
Until/till
But
Because

At that moment
... who ...   ... when ...
... that ...   ... where ...
... or ...   ... happily ever after
... so that ...

'Run' (he walked and he walked ...)
Description – a lean cat ...
Alliteration
Simile – using 'as'
Adjectives to describe
Adverbs: Luckily/unfortunately, suddenly, immediately
Prepositions: down, into, over, out, onto, inside, towards

Suddenly
To his amazement
After/after that
So
By the next morning
If
Now
Soon/ as soon as
In the end
Finally

Introduce

although
however

... to ...

Repetition for effect
Adjectives to describe
Adverbs: eventually
Prepositions
Simile using 'like'

Action bank

Key connective	Suggested action
Once upon a time	open hands like a book.
Early one morning	hands to one side of head and pretend to wake up.
Who	finger circle index finger in air.
First	one finger up.
Next	2 fingers pointed to one side.
But	fingers down.
Because	hands out open palmed.
At that moment	
Suddenly	hands expressively open as if in surprise.
To his amazement	
Unfortunately	
Luckily	hands raised open as if thanking.
After/after that	roll hands over in turning gesture.
So	roll hands forwards and open as if giving.
Finally	Palm facing audience like a policeman stopping traffic
In the end	bring hands together as if closing book.
Eventually	

Appendices

Reception Stories	Language features	Imitation	Innovation	Invention
The Little Red Hen The Gingerbread man The Enormous turnip The Billy goats Gruff Going for a song Peter and the wolf Cumulative stories Journey/quest stories Problem/resolution stories Wishing tales Beating the Baddie Warning story Success Criteria: By the end of the year pupils should be able to select and retell a whole story from a bank of well-known tales either in the original form or own simple innovation.	Once upon a time Early one morning And Then Next Until/till But So Finally ... who ... • 'Run' (he walked and he walked)+repetitive pattern; • Description – a lean cat, a mean cat ... • Alliteration • Adverbs: • Luckily/unfortunately • Prepositions: down, into, over, out, onto. • Full stops	• children join in with story, using actions; • simple story map used; • teacher withdraws from telling; • story circles and pairs; • acting out of story and other classroom activities to make story memorable • independent retelling of story; • daily spelling and sentence games.	• Whole class innovations; • Individual/paired innovations – story map, actions and retelling. • *Substitutions*: simple, non-chronological changes; • *Addition*: adding in descriptive details to character or settings; add new events following a set pattern; • *Alteration*: occasional alteration that has consequences; change ending; • daily spelling and sentence games.	• Whole class inventions; • Pair/individual inventions – using story maps, actions and retelling. • Simple stories based on: Once upon a time One morning Unfortunately Luckily So Finally ... • simple journey stories; • simple cumulative, patterned stories; • stories based on other stories; • problem/resolution stories; • stories about own life. • daily spelling and sentence games.

Year 1 Stories	Language features	Imitation	Innovation	Invention
Monkey see – Monkey do! The 3 Bears The 3 little pigs The Magic Porridge Pot How tortoise got his shell Rumplestiltskin Trickster tale Cumulative stories Journey/quest stories Problem/resolution stories 'How' myth Wishing tales Beating the Baddie Success criteria: By the end of the year pupils should be able to retell a whole, known tale or innovation with substitution and simple addition as well as retelling own invented story.	Once upon a time One day – Early one morning First Next Until/till Then And ... so ... but ... because ... if ... when Now By the next morning If At that moment – Suddenly – To his amazement After/after that Soon/ as soon as So Because But In the end – Finally ... who ... ... when ... ... that ... ... where ... ... or ... ... so that ... ... happily ever after • 'Run' (he walked and he walked ...) • Description – a lean cat ... • Alliteration • Simile – using 'as' • Adjectives to describe • Adverbs: Luckily/unfortunately, suddenly, immediately; • Prepositions: down, into, over, out, onto, inside, towards • Full stops and capitals.	• children join in with story, using actions; • simple story map used; • teacher withdraws from telling; • acting out of story and other classroom activities to make story memorable; • story circles and pairs; • daily retelling; • independent retelling of story; • daily spelling and sentence games. • sound punctuation for some stories. *Sentence types:* Simple and compound sentences; Complex sentences using connectives; Questions and exclamations; Long and short sentences; Repetitive patterns. *Sentence openers:* When – time connective How – adverb, e.g. suddenly, unfortunately, luckily.	• Whole class innovations; • Individual/paired innovations – story map, actions and retelling. • *Substitutions:* simple, non-chronological changes, e.g. character, place, objects; • *Addition:* adding in descriptive details to character or settings; add new events following a set pattern; embellish sentences. • *Alteration:* occasional alteration in middle that has consequences; change ending; • *Change of view:* retell part of a story from a character's view, e.g. hot seating. • daily spelling and sentence games.	• Whole class inventions; • Pair/individual inventions – using story maps, actions and retelling; • Simple stories: beginning, middle and end using connectives, e.g. • Once upon a time • One day • Next • Suddenly • Luckily • finally • telling, retelling and drawing before writing; • introduce principle of '3'; • simple journey, cumulative, problem/resolution stories; stories based on objects, pictures, puppets, etc; stories based on other stories • stories about own life. • daily spelling and sentence games.

Year 2	Language features	Imitation	Innovation	Invention
The Papaya that spoke How the World was made Cat, Bramble and Heron Mr Fox and his bag The Magic Brush The Hobyahs Trickster tale Cumulative stories Journey/quest stories Problem/resolution stories 'How' myth Wishing tales Magic stories Beating the Baddie Success criteria: By the end of the year pupils should be able to retell a whole, known tale or innovation with substitution, addition, alteration of ending and other events as well as retelling own invented whole story with defined beginning, middle and ending, using story language.	Once upon a time One day – Early one morning First Next Until/till Then And ... so ... but ... because ... if ... when Now By the next morning If At that moment – Suddenly – To his amazement However/ Although After/after that Soon/ as soon as So Because But In the end – Finally *Sentence types:* Simple and compound sentences; Complex sentences using connectives; Questions and exclamations; Long and short sentences; dialogue Repetitive patterns; Descriptive lists, e.g. he wore old shoes, a dark cloak and a red hat ... *Sentence openers:* When – time connective How – adverb, e.g. suddenly, unfortunately, luckily. Where – e.g. Across the road ... • ... who ... when ... ... that ... where ... ...or ... to ... so that ... ...happily ever after • 'Run' (he walked and he walked ...) • Description – a lean cat ... • Alliteration • Simile – using 'as'; using 'like' • Adjectives to describe • Adverbs: Luckily/unfortunately, suddenly, immediately; • Prepositions: down, into, over, out, onto, inside, towards • Full stops, capitals, question/ exclamation marks, commas in list, speech marks.	• children join in with story, using actions and story map; • teacher withdraws; • acting out of story and classroom activities to make story memorable; • story circles and pairs; • daily retelling; • independent retelling of story; • daily spelling and sentence games.	• Whole class, individual/paired innovations – story map, actions and retelling. • *Substitutions:* simple changes, e.g. character, place, objects; • *Addition:* adding in descriptive details to character or settings; add new events or characters; embellish sentences; add dialogue. • *Alteration:* alteration in middle that has consequences; change ending; alter a character's disposition and change setting. • *Change of view:* retell part of a story from a character's view, e.g. hot seating. • *Recycle basic plot:* to create a new story. • daily spelling and sentence games.	• Whole class inventions; • Pair/individual inventions – using story maps, actions and retelling; • Simple stories based on: opening, build up, dilemma, resolution, ending, using connectives; • telling, retelling and drawing before writing; • re-use known plots to create own tales; • reflect taught sentence features in own compositions; • draw on bank of known stories, reading and own life including new ideas; • principle of '3'; • control inventions using story maps, mountains or boards to plan; • daily spelling and sentence games.

Appendices

Resources

Rhymes for learning
* The Works Key Stage 1, edited Pie Corbett, Macmillan Children's Books – a large collection of nursery rhymes, action/playground rhymes, skipping, clapping and circle rhymes that are all out of copyright.

A few useful books
- The Ladybird 'favourite tales' series has over 30 traditional tales.
- The Nursery Tales, retold by Brian Morse – Ladybird.
- The Helen Oxenbury Nursery Story Book – Young Lions
- Barefoot Books – beautiful traditional tales collections worth buying.
- The Magic Lands retold by Kevin Crossley-Holland – Orion.
- English Fairy Tales, retold by Joseph Jacobs – Puffin Books.
- Traditional storytelling in the primary classroom – a very handy and practical book – by Teresa Grainger – Scholastic.
- The Story Making Framework – the original planning framework and account of the research carried out by the International Learning and Research Centre is available by writing to: ILRC, North St, Oldland Common, South Gloucestershire BS30 8TL

Feltboards and figures: www.edufun.co.uk

Web sites: mainly for teachers – do check them.

www.bbc.co.uk/cbeebies/storycircle/fairystories
Illustrated site with some interactive stories.

www.storyarts.org/lessonplans/lessonideas/index.html
Lesson ideas and other activities such as treasure hunts.

www.sfs.org.uk
The website of the Society for Storytelling.

www.scottishstorytellingcentre.org.uk/
The Scottish storytelling centre.

www.pjtss.net/ring/
The website of the 'Storytelling Ring' has over a hundred links.

This story could be used with any age group. I have attached a story map so you can see what it might look like!

Kassim and the hungry Fox

Once upon a time there was a little boy called Kassim who lived in the middle of big city.

Early one morning he woke up and set off to the bakers to buy a loaf of fresh bread and a lemon pie for tea. But his Mummy warned him, 'Watch out for the fox!'

Next he walked, jiggety-jog, jiggety-jog, jiggety-jog till he came to a long, dark alleyway. Woof! There he met a dog – with a swishing, twitching tail!

'I'm hungry,' said the dog. 'What have you got in your bag?'

'Nothing,' said Kassim, 'But follow me, I'm going to the bakers.'

So Kassim and the dog walked, jiggety-jog, jiggety-jog, jiggety-jog till they came to the market square. Meeow! There they met a cat – with bright green eyes.

'I'm hungry,' said the cat. 'What have you got in your bag?'

'Nothing,' said Kassim, 'But follow me, I'm going to the bakers.'

So Kassim and the dog and the cat walked, jiggety-jog, jiggety-jog, jiggety-jog till they came to the old well. Eeeeeek! There they met a rat – with long silvery whiskers.

'I'm hungry,' said the rat. 'What have you got in your bag?'

'Nothing,' said Kassim, 'But follow me, I'm going to the bakers.'

So Kassim and the dog and the cat and the rat walked, jiggety-jog, jiggety-jog, jiggety-jog till they came to the baker's shop.

Unfortunately, the shop was closed!

To their surprise, they met a fox – a lean fox with mean eyes!

'I'm hungry,' said the fox. 'Follow me.' Unfortunately, Kassim, the dog, the cat and the rat followed the fox, jiggety-jog, jiggety-jog, jiggety-jog till they came to the fox's den.

'I'm so hungry, do come in for a bite,' said the fox, licking his lips ...

Luckily,
the rat went EEEK,
the cat went MEOW
the dog went WOOF,
and Kassim shouted, 'NOW – RUN!'

So they ran and they ran and they ran, jiggety-jog, jiggety-jog, jiggety-jog all the way back to Kassim's house, where his Mother told them how silly they had been, but then gave them each a nice slice of orange pie for tea!

Story Map

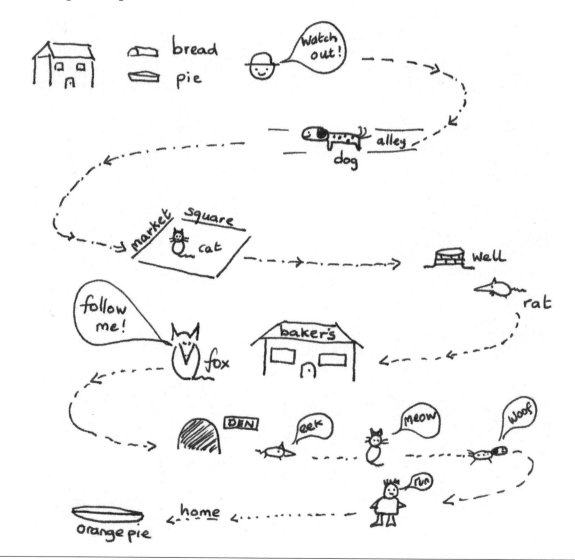